THE
PAINTER'S
MIND

THE PAINTER'S MIND

A Study of the
Relations of Structure
and Space
in Painting

by

ROMARE BEARDEN
and CARL HOLTY

Crown Publishers, Inc., New York

LIBRARY OF CONGRESS CATALOG CARD NUMBER: 75–75067
PRINTED IN THE UNITED STATES OF AMERICA
Published simultaneously in Canada by
General Publishing Company Limited
Designed by Shari de Miskey

Contents

Preface

Many students who were nurtured on the notion of self-expression as the sole criterion for integrated painting are now seeking a more precise knowledge of their craft; and many art lovers, seeking an extra dimension to their appreciation of fine art, would still like to understand two of the most fundamental aspects of any painting—structure and space. "How is a painting put together?"—that is the question that still troubles art students, art lovers, and amateur and professional painters alike.

THE PAINTER'S MIND is addressed to precisely this question, elucidating the manual and visual aspects of a great variety of different kinds and genres of painting, and stressing not a mechanical application of rules but that visual judgment needed to make a free choice about space and structure.

Each concept is demonstrated with drawings and analyses of important works of art. And the demonstrations are direct, not the mysterious collections of circles and triangles so often seen in other books and articles on composition. The nature of pictorial space and structure is clearly defined, and the space of painting is differentiated from that of our everyday world; in fact, space is shown to be the end result of the interrelatedness of all the structural elements.

7

Though this is not a book of art history, we do hope to
clarify certain continuities in the long history of picturemaking
by describing various spatial and structural methods employed
by the great painters—painters who nevertheless worked, for
the most part, in different stylistic conventions. We hope also
that by relating our technical discussion with some of the
social and aesthetic thinking which gave it rise and direction
the reader will have a better understanding of the painter and
his problems.

In addition, THE PAINTER'S MIND should offer a fresh approach to many painting problems and, concomitantly, an
opportunity for others to reexamine some of their own concepts.
Since painting is always about something—a painter's vision of
the world—a painter's accomplishments are often restricted by
his knowledge and taste; this book will be instructive because
even the most gifted artist must give careful and continuing
thought to the problems of pictorial space and structure.

Curiously, there are any number of books such as ours in the
fields of poetry, prose fiction, and music, where it is not at all
unusual to analyze structure and the principles of composition.
There are precious few for painting—and the resistance to such
books has been as long as it is unfortunate and misguided.

I

The
Painter's
Mind

Although the emphasis in this book will be on methods, we are not blind to the soaring spirit of each true artist, and to his deep and important subjective drives. As painters, we have spent enough hours of self-searching to be aware of how much of creation lies within the unfathomable wellsprings of the artist's character and mind—forces over which he often has too little direct control.

We too have struggled, not only with the stubbornly unsympathetic mediums of the painter—which he must master or at least come to terms with—but with the creative urge that must be directed toward a rationale of order. We have felt it thwart our every effort; we have felt it turn impishly into that old malaise of the artist, creative anxiety.

Artists, from times long past to the present day, have suffered the anxieties of this mystery—and each in his own way has sought to attain a totality of expression. Yet in spite of the fact that no artist ever has, or ever will, completely discipline this condition, an alarming number of artists in this century, supported by their own rather pragmatic interpretations of modern psychology and science, attempted to settle the problem of creative anxiety by simply denying its existence. It is therefore natural that these persons should look upon what art history and tradition have to teach as a seductive trap—a trap that would land them in the dread floundering with problems of drawing and painting and in the misery of interpreting their personal feelings. Also, they are convinced that they already know all they need to know about "how pictures are put together." Have not a thousand lectures on "art appreciation" provided them with this knowledge?

Curiously, the genesis of this thinking occurred at a time when the subjective attitude was in ascendency. Many of the Abstract Expressionists attempted to break all ties with the past and, like the hero of E. M. Forster's novel, *Howards End,* they wished to come upon art as the revivalist seeks to discover Christ.

What is it in our fast-changing world that causes each successive generation to become so dissatisfied with every aspect of the preceding generation? With all the initial drumbeating for Abstract Expressionism as America's first artistic export, the ideology collapsed after a few years; and almost overnight the gallery-goers found on the walls of their favorite galleries enlargements of their children's favorite comic strips, soup cans, and multiple images of Marilyn Monroe, instead of the pulsating color rhythms of the Abstract Expressionists. At least, though, most of the new formalists of the hard-edge and minimal art groups remain faithful to the belief that art is born of conceptual innocence. Thus the artists of the not-so-distant past and those of the present hold aloft, between them, the banner of *"un art autre"* (that art other than any that preceded it), a term attributed to the noted critic Michel Tapié. In contrast, one remembers how Renoir became, at forty, disaffected with Impressionist theories and practices, and confessed: "I feel as though I had to learn to draw and paint all over again."

Together with these periodic states of dissatisfaction, we find artists constantly changing to a new manner of working. Such changes are often occasioned by reasons other than a genuine inspiration for new ideas. Each movement produces only a few artists favored by public attention and acclaim; others may be tolerated during the period when their particular movement enjoys prestige, but when the general enthusiasm wanes these artists are often unjustly dismissed as hangers-on. It is at this point, when artists of some accomplishment, who feel they have not received the attention and material rewards that their works merit, sometimes attempt a new manner of working.

By no means are we referring only to artists of the contemporary scene; in fact, a change of artistic activity, a switch over to another way of thinking, was within the daily order of the Renaissance. Brunelleschi, a first-rate sculptor, abandoned that art after losing to Ghiberti the competition to execute the portals of the Florentine priory. He then left Florence for Rome where he engaged himself as an architect. Leonardo da Vinci went to Milan to take service with the local tyrant, the Duke of Sforza, as a fortifications engineer, after he had somehow escaped the favorable attention of the Medicis. Students of that era quickly learned their craft and often were chosen over their teachers for the lucrative commissions, because they were more willing to make the kinds of concessions that would please their patrons. When Raphael's master, Perugino, fell behind in popular taste and lost out on commissions he was left disconsolate, and, in the end, he died impoverished and abandoned by those who owed him so much as their former teacher and mentor.

In contrast to such acts of self-interest, we know that Rembrant made an artistic outlaw of himself by pursuing his aim, as he put it, to become a painter rather than a cloth dyer.

Eschewing the acceptable and profitable style of his early portraits, Rembrandt soon learned the price he would have to pay for his artistic freedom; yet he never swerved from his self-appointed way.

What inspires an artist? Who can say for sure that it is one thing or another, one person or another? Who can rule out even the most impossible or seeming impertinent considerations?

Although the lives of most well-known artists are adequately documented, those very things which inspired them to become and then remain artists are the most elusive and enigmatic. When we think of an artist's earliest days (perhaps as early as childhood, certainly in youth), André Malraux's comments seem to come closest to the truth: the young artist, he said, is attracted to art through art—that is, he is inspired by seeing pictures, good or bad. It is doubtful that he is inspired at first by some attractive aspect in nature—the ubiquitous sunset, for example—until he has seen a painted picture of it by some artist.

In a whimsical bit of testimony during his lawsuit against Ruskin, Whistler told the court that he was born in St. Petersburg; although he spent some time there as a youth, Whistler was actually born in Lowell, Massachusetts. His whimsy supports Malraux's contention, for what Whistler had in mind was his first visit to the famous Hermitage Museum; it was at this time that his life became really meaningful for him. And in another discipline, more closely related to art than one might believe, it has been well established that Sir Isaac Newton was first led to study mathematics through an interest in astrology. To try to understand some astrological diagrams, he purchased a book on trigonometry. This led to an interest in geometry that continued until he had mastered all the mathematics of his day and finally, almost simultaneously with Leibnitz, invented the calculus.

But after the call to the profession, anything might act as a stimulus—even a sunset—for there are enough fine paintings of this subject by Turner, Lorraine, and others to prove this is so. At the other extreme, the modern painter and sculptor Jean Arp, in composing a series of works, let some pieces of paper fall at random upon a surface and afterward traced the papers where they had fallen as his germinal source for these paintings. But the great landscape painter John Constable, in his lecture notes on the use of figures to enliven a landscape, advises the artist not to introduce imagined figures but to wait for a real horse or a real man to appear as a model, for "there is no corner in our lovely England so remote but what some living being will walk right into the composition."

Popular novels and motion pictures with an artist as hero never fail to develop a deep romantic attraction for the girl of the artist's dreams as the *sine qua non* of artistic inspiration. Silly? Perhaps. Yet think of how deeply interwoven the works of Picasso are with the women in his life, even if he seems not to act out the role of ever-faithful lover depicted in novels and movies. And think of the way his countryman Goya proclaimed, in a group of outstanding paintings, his love for the Duchess of Alba and his pride in that clandestine relationship.

Sometimes the poet can divine truths in the varied promptings and motivations of the artist with more cogency than the historian or critic. In his romance on Leonardo, the novelist Merezhkovski has the artist say of a portrait he is about to undertake (which we now know as the *Mona Lisa*): "It befell me to make a beautiful picture." Though Leonardo probably never said such a thing, it is a noble invention, much in keeping with the painter's towering spirit; and there are remarks in Leonardo's notebooks that give plausibility to Merezhkovski's poetry as truthful to the intent of that great genius of the Renaissance.

It is not idle daydreaming to imagine oneself in another time and place, to try to become—if only for a moment—an artist of the past or one of his contemporaries. Through such projection, one might well find out how the great ones faced many of the same problems artists confront today. For a modern student to realize that the slouching nude model in the depressing art school studio is related to those from whom some of the greatest masters worked, and undoubtedly resented as much by the student of today, is to find a positive empathy with the past. A famous professor of ancient history once told his students that all their attempts to conceive the life of Rome, in the days of the Caesars, would be inadequate unless they could imagine two senators on the Capitol steps telling each other the latest stories about the farmer's daughter.

An educator once described the development in painting over the past 150 years as beginning with a preoccupation with the object (Academicism and Realism), progressing through an evolution that embodied the achievement of placing that object in space (Cubism), and culminating in an ultimate effort that dealt with space itself (neo-Plasticism).

This is an oversimplification.

If all were that simple, the new and further reduced hard-edge abstraction and minimal art paintings would be the obvious conclusion; and the final step to environmental art would be short and logical. But in spite of what the purists may claim, purely aesthetic concerns are always allied with problems of subjectivity and of subject matter. The desire to consider art as dealing only with art cannot exclude the artist, or all the things that affect him. So Tachisme and much of Abstract Expressionism, where the language and idiom are realized in dealing with the space itself, cannot be limited to such systems of space as scientists calculate, nor are we able to regard these artists with just dispassionate interest.

The most "classical" works in all the arts of the last two centuries are, to a great degree, romantic. Seurat, for instance, sharply disclaimed all subjective interest in his subject matter, yet Professor Robert Herbert of Yale University, who recently published a fine book of drawings by this artist, sees him as a socially conscious painter—that is, an artist engaged in the social problems of his time.

Artists are inspired and repelled by their immediate fore-bears, and react to their examples in the manner that best serves their own interests and needs. If a direct continuity with what these predecessors have begun seems fruitful, the artists will often continue the tradition. But if a particular source of creativity seems to have nothing more to offer, artists will turn elsewhere: to past times, perhaps; away from art altogether (Dada); to a new psychology; to science; to litera-ture, music, or religion; to the social problems of the day; to nature—all in an attempt to find somewhere the proper inspira-tion for their art.

Matisse, referring to his youth and his personal association with Impressionist and post-Impressionist masters (Degas, Pissarro, Signac), wrote that despite the vitality of those artists he found it necessary to go into the distant past to find the means through which he could develop his own work. He did not *imitate* the Persian miniaturists or the Greek vase painters. He studied them; then he created out of his own vision. Today, preoccupied with "self-expression" as we are, it is almost an irony that this joyous and seemingly spontaneous artist should have been one of the most methodical masters of all time. Yet he emphasized his logical and methodical procedure in numer-ous interviews with others and particularly in the catalogue introduction of his 1948 exhibition in Philadelphia, which he seems to have written with young artists in mind.

Artists in our time are generally reluctant to consult the writings of earlier artists. Perhaps this is because what the older artists wrote was in fact limited to their times, or that some of the writing was actually inconsistent with their actual practices. Renoir, for instance, advised young artists to study from nature; but he learned most of the real essentials of paint-ing by studying at the Louvre.

Henri Matisse, *The Purple Robe. The Baltimore Museum of Art, The Cone Collection*

Leonardo, in his *Journals,* deals with the particular interest he had in the study of nature, rather than with the general problems of picturemaking. He was especially interested in broadening the overall vision of the Renaissance, and in his paintings and drawings he incorporated his detailed knowledge of nature. Van Gogh, in his letters, constantly reveals his subjective way of seeing "nature through the eyes of the personality." And Mondrian, whose aim it was to see through nature, especially certain aspects of its structure, wrote of his researches in the spirit of a philosopher; he gave very little technical information regarding his methods of work.

Ultimately, what is most revealing is the work of art itself. Perhaps the day will come when each artist will be completely devoid of any traditional influence and will exist on his own little island of space; but until then, the historical figures we study in this book, as well, of course, as many others, had ancestors. They also have descendants. Consequently, they (and we) were not forced to learn and solve complex problems of space and structure by themselves. And these great figures of the past still have much to tell us—as mentors, perhaps, rather than as schoolteachers—even though most of what they have to impart is nonverbal.

Harry Holtzman, in speaking of the corrections that Rembrandt made on the drawings of his students, said that the message is so clear it fairly shouts at you. Yes, how clearly Rembrandt in all of his drawings emphasizes the big movements of the plane and the spatial areas, with broad strokes of his sepia or ink-loaded brush, never descending to the particular but always concerned with the most essential structural elements. And, as Holtzman implied, how rewarding it still is to study these masterful drawings.

The totality, or total unity, of a work of art does not inhibit it from moving us emotionally. What a complete work of art does is to limit our emotional response in scope and in kind.

It demands of the observer a participation and relieves that observer of the often rather arduous efforts of identification; but it also demands a certain humility, and a willingness to submit to a change within oneself.

An incomplete work of art, however, can also evoke an emotional response like that of a cry in the still night, the sound of an explosion, the confused alarms following an accident—and these impressions, gathered from some shocking experience, are neither as shallow nor as superficial as some people may believe. A room long inhabited by someone who has died, for example, will seem to retain a memory of the deceased for a long time afterward. Often someone can tell at a glance whether the confusion in a room, with all of its appointments in disarray, was caused by an intruder, an act of nature, or by an untidy person. A section of material onto which paint has been dropped will be of an entirely different nature, depending upon whether the paint was dripped by an artist in the process of creation or by a house painter using the material as a floor covering. But with time these purely emotional experiences vanish from our consciousness. The felt presence in the room fades away. What caused the disorder in the room becomes irrelevant. And except for the work of a few rare painters, we need not concern ourselves with whether the blots of paint are by design or accident.

Though some of these events are disturbing, we have had an encounter that has moved us to an inner response. Sensibility and imagination were both involved and the intensity of the experience may even have been acute. But the events were not art. They were fragmented experiences—fleeting, confused, even inchoate. They did not evoke the response one has when he is confronted by a work in which all the parts are related, a work that must be considered on its own terms. This difference is not generally understood. There are many people, in fact, who whether they understand it or not, still insist that the art experience be the same as the life experience.

Robert C. Scull, a prominent art collector, recently wrote: "I judge art, not by history, but by the measure of my response and personal involvement in the art experience." Later in his article, "A Collector's Notes," printed in the Metropolitan Museum of Art's *Bulletin,* Mr. Scull refers to a specific picture he had purchased, stating that it "speaks to all mankind, employing the plain language of everyday man, not the secret signs of the specialist."

The collector makes his position clear enough, though his attitude is the very epitome of the desire to partake and identify but not to participate. This attitude also defines much of the increased art activity, not only in the United States but the world over. We read constantly about programs fashioned to encourage art—though, interestingly, most of them are similar to those planned during the 1930's.

There is no doubt that the progress of culture was interrupted during the Depression years and World War II, although it is true that a good number of young soldiers were brought into direct contact with art as they passed through the large cities both here and in Europe. The present expansion of educational institutions, museums, and art schools would be frightening were this expansion not so welcome. And allied with such activities, there is now a worldwide participation in all of the modern styles of painting and sculpture—a participation without precedence.

But it is one thing to become acquainted with the humanities, another to really understand them. To go from immediate and narrow enthusiasm to broad and deep understanding requires that a person seek out and even master the knowledge of the disciplines that interest him. Talent, genius, and the mystery of the personality, however, are neither so easily understood nor so easily husbanded.

But in spite of this, THE PAINTER'S MIND should be of much value and pertinence to the interested reader. We mentioned that artists in the past often wrote of their craft in the most general terms—a phenomenon sometimes occasioned by the fact that as members of various painters' guilds, had they divulged secret formulas and painting methods they would most certainly have been expelled from the guilds, and in some instances actually garroted.

Today we are safe enough on that score!

Then, too, with the development of the modern movement and the perpetual assessment of those things essential and non-essential to painting and sculpture, artists have dispensed with a great clutter of irrelevancies. In his *Journal*, even so comparatively modern a painter as Eugène Delacroix writes of the attention he paid to the centering of important personages in his compositions, and to the details of dress, gesture, expression, human and animal anatomy, and perspective. The famous salon painter of the nineteenth century, Meissonier, had a group of horsemen ride through a field so that he could be aided in painting a battle scene involving a great cavalry charge. However, what will always be essential in any work of art are the image and structure—and neither of these facets can be supplied solely by the imagination of even the most sympathetic observer.

Many things are revealed to us as we look at a work of art, with its multiplicity of images. Not all who look see the same thing; some people, for instance, will be pleased by a particular image, others depressed—each according to his temperament, his imagination, and his spiritual needs. But whatever the image, the only visual reality present is the structure. There is no real face, no real ship, no real landscape, no real depth. These are illusions; the structure that supports them is not. Since it is the structure that provides the image with a sense of reality, we can even refer to such different artists as Courbet and Mondrian as Realists.

Though the separation of space from structure must be arbitrary, we will of necessity treat them separately to facilitate analysis. Compared to the contemplation of structure, the spatial concept of an art work is relatively easier to isolate since, visually, it is more in evidence. However, spatial involvement itself can be interpreted in many different ways. An artist of our acquaintance once spoke of the dramatic manner in which the planes in Mondrian's neo-Plastic paintings advanced and receded. When he was advised that such an effect was hardly possible (since Mondrian neither desired nor intended such an illusion, and indeed had expended great creativity in keeping each plane within the frontal tension of one plane) our friend replied that Mondrian had simply failed to take into account his capacity for hallucination!

Though the painter's mind is infinitely varied and will be inspired, will flourish, and will mature under a host of differing stimuli and actions, we are convinced that Malraux's principle, "art through art," remains of paramount importance. The lawfulness of art, as embodied in a representative group of paintings, is our concern in this book. Naturally, the painter's mind is most truly reflected in the works he has created.

Thus, it is not the artist but the work that reveals the truth in art. A simple visual fact such as a plane of color, a simple or even complex shape, the representation of a nude figure or a landscape or a bridge or even a sunset—none of these is, in itself, a truth. And they are not art. Art and truth are arrived at through the relationships in any painting and must be understood not in terms of the world in which we live—rather, within the world of the work itself.

The understanding of art is in good part an understanding of the relationships within a painting—relationships that we will now examine closely within the context of our two principal concerns here, structure and space.

II

Structure

THE FORMULATION OF THE SPATIAL ELEMENTS INTO A UNIFIED WHOLE

The structure of a work of art is all-embracing. It must encompass the subject matter, theme, and aesthetic aspirations as well as the means by which the artist's intentions are realized. True artistic structure differs from those simple construction or layout methods which, for most part, derive from a systematized logic. In books on composition, one often reads such statements as: "This picture is composed within a triangular shape," and "the Holy Family is set within an arrangement of ovals." These observations refer only to the surface layout of the picture.

UNITY

Let's clarify this principle of a unified structure, and differentiate it from a construction or layout method.

Books on grammar detail methods for planning a composition; arrangements for preparing an initial outline are presented, so that one's ideas can be developed with continuity and coherence. The outline, however, represents only the skeletal part of the overall composition. With a good writer, the unified structure of the completed work has rhythm and variety in every sentence and paragraph, and the writer's style bears relation to his thinking and subject matter; everything strives toward a unity of purpose and execution.

Similarly, in the execution of the old Byzantine and pre-Renaissance mosaics, the relations of color, accent, and volume were worked out in the actual placement of the stones. Here, not only rhythm and drama, but the structural control was also established. The very choice of the colors, the particular color areas, and the outline of the shapes actually evolved in the process of the painting. Because of this method, the art of mosaic itself is referred to as painting. The mosaic could be considered as finished only when the final pieces of tesserae had been placed—just as a painting by such great colorists as Titian, Monet, and Cézanne reached completion only with the final brushstrokes.

The various methods of unifying paintings were first conceived with works of reasonable, nonmonumental dimensions in mind. The late Ad Reinhardt decided, at a mature point in his career, that a canvas measuring 60 $\times$ 60 inches was the proper scale for his works because of its relationship to physical man himself. The concept of *la mesure humaine*—the equation between the size of an art object and the dimension of man—was of course not originated by Reinhardt, though it is possible that the exact dimension he used was derived by him. Vitruvius, for example, explained that the development of the Dorian column was based on the measure of a man's foot; the length of a man's foot is roughly one sixth his height, and, in accord with this ratio, the shaft of the column was erected to a height of six times that of the base. Many of Reinhardt's predecessors considered a canvas up to ten feet in its largest dimensions to be within the human scale because this, when one stood some distance from the work, approached in the mind's eye the size of man.

Though the problem of unity may begin with scale, however, its solutions are all internal—and thus similar regardless of the physical size of the area of the canvas.

Each painter faces the same problems of unity. Accordingly, painters have contrived construction methods as an aid in composing their paintings. There are many such methods. Here is one used by certain Dutch landscape painters during the seventeenth and eighteenth centuries.

Initially, the canvas was divided into one area for the lights and another for the darks. As the painting progressed, if a dark color were moved into the lighter section (such as a tree projecting above the horizon) a balancing light color would be introduced into the darker area—a cow, for instance, or a figure clothed in a light garment. By continuing this procedure the painters were able to achieve some degree of mechanical balance between light and dark. Cuyp, Ruisdael, and Hobbema used this method in varying degrees.

Terborch, de Hooch, and Vermeer—called the "Little Dutch Masters" because of the small size of their paintings—worked with more complex problems in structure, yet they were able to integrate the visual objects, and, in fact, all the subject matter into the pictorial structure of their paintings. In order to do so, they had to devise means whereby the objects, the figures, and the linear perspective could be brought into relationship with the rectangular, almost geometric, structure of the total painting. In such paintings of this school as de Hooch's *Interior with Young Couple,* one can often observe how the directionals of the perspective are dissolved within subtle patterns of light and shadow that pass across the picture. Sometimes the figures are set in similar rectangles, with the faces, arms, and legs of the figures conceived as but slight deviations from the overall geometrical structure.

It might be noted that this school of painting reveals the basis for Mondrian's Cubism, which is structurally based on subdivisions of the planes that parallel the four sides, with

Jan Vermeer, *Girl Interrupted at Her Music. The Frick Collection, New York*

Pieter de Hooch, *Interior with Young Couple. The Metropolitan Museum of Art. Bequest of Benjamin Altman, 1913*

Portrait said to be Taira-no-Shigemari, and attributed to Fujiwara Taka-nobu. *Courtesy Jingo-ji-Kyoto, Japan*

contrasts in size and position. Although diagonals are sometimes used as guides in the placement of the planes, these
artists do not proceed by the superimposition of planes placed
diagonally across the surface—a method often used by Picasso
and several other Cubists, as well as by Takanobu, the great
Japanese painter who might be called an early proto-Cubist.
And in an interesting way, the use of photographs and other
materials, set into apparently unrelated shapes in some of the
modern montage pictures, reminds us of the methods of de
Hooch—though he, of course, was not interested in the shock
value, or any other modern purpose, for the montage. De
Hooch is especially interesting for the way he unites diverse
and apparently contradictory elements within his paintings.

Quite another method can be seen in the frescoes of Andrea
del Castagno. Not long after World War II a fresco was removed from the supporting wall, revealing Castagno's simple,
sepia-outlined drawing underneath. Refined in unity and resolution, this drawing served as the layout or guide for the
composition. The enrichment and unification of the fresco was
developed during the actual painting.

Many young artists often find it difficult to achieve a convincing structure because structural concerns often seem to be
so far apart from the images that animate their dreams—no
matter whether the effects they desire are representational or
decorative in nature. In the world of actual appearances we
can tell if a man is seated in a chair; but in the world of painting, the seated man can be made convincing only when the
structure supporting the image is in itself convincing. Velásquez, like many other Spanish painters, painted a series of
portraits of Philip IV, of whom, of course, we have no photographs; yet, as Picasso remarked, it is Velásquez's version of
the King that we have accepted, not those of other painters.
Certainly, one reason for this is that they hold structurally as
greater paintings. It is possible, however, that some of the
other artists achieved a more truthful likeness.

Synòpia for Castagno's *The Resurrection. Uffizi, Florence* >

Andrea del Castagno, *The Resurrection. Uffizi, Florence*

Velásquez, *Philip IV of Spain. The Frick Collection, New York*

In a like manner, the young artist will register his intentions only if the ornaments are realized within a structure that will provide a proper equilibrium for their relationships. So much of the current work of reduction, as we see it in the so-called hard-edged style, or in Abstract Expressionism, fails to attain such a balance, or equilibrium. In many instances the painters refer to a faulty area in their painting as a section that "is not working"; thus the error is equated with a subjective moment of weakness—not to a lack of pictorial understanding.

With a convincing structure there are seldom contradictions between the artist's intentions and his method of realization; as Coleridge wrote, "No work of true genius dares want its appropriate form." When structural contradictions do exist, the composition of the art form is not persuasive, no matter how well it is executed technically. The nineteenth century, more than any other, offers conspicuous examples of these contradictions. There were many painters who attempted to use some of the principles of Impressionism in projecting the lifeless content of their salon pieces, or in painting the pictorial content of past decades. A Madonna or a saint, partly depicted in the scientific light of Impressionism and partly in the academic, was not credible in either style. An artist can study other styles, but to work effectively he must deal with the structural methods that are valid for his time.

Just one glance at the commercial liturgical painting of the last century, as seen in the work of a painter like Anton Hoffman and even in the work of the much more admirable Albert Weisgerber who painted a St. Sebastian in the Impressionist manner, will give proof of this dichotomy in structure.

But Matisse, who derived much of his drawing style from a study of the linear paintings on Greek vases and his color from Persian prints, successfully applied this knowledge to his own painting and drawing. Whether in the more decorative and monumental painting of his earlier and last styles, or in the odalisques and still lifes of his middle years, Matisse drew neither Greek vases nor Persian prints. His accomplishment was to absorb these influences into one of the most personal visions of the twentieth century.

In our time, certain artists have adopted Cubistic methods to provide a modern format for concepts essentially illustrative. There is, for example, that painting of a symphony orchestra (reproductions of which are often seen in printshops) conceived quite academically yet, in what must have been an afterthought, the painter has cut up the figures and background into bizarre, unrelated triangles. Recently, David Parks, Asger Jorn, and others tried to create figural images out of the free forms of Abstract Expressionism, but the truncated freaks and vague figures that supposedly are bathers and nudes do not attain credibility.

TASTE

In achieving a convincing structure, the question of taste in painting is always of great significance; the painter, and also the viewer, must choose between what is "right" and what is not. The model that Rembrandt used for *Bathsheba* is a woman that few would consider pretty, yet that painter's perfect organization of the picture offers sensations that only true beauty can evoke. J. L. Gérôme, in *Roman Slave Market*, shows the back of a beautiful girl; however, the banality of the pictorial content overwhelms the observer, drawing attention to the yawning background spaces and away from the girl. Even the girl's prettiness becomes transient because of the painter's lack of taste and artistic response. We see her head cushioned in a white shoulder that is, in reality, not a shoulder at all. No one questions the rightness, however, of the woman's hands in the Rembrandt, despite their extravagant scale in relation to the head.

J. L. Gérôme, *The Roman Slave Market. The Walters Art Gallery, Baltimore*

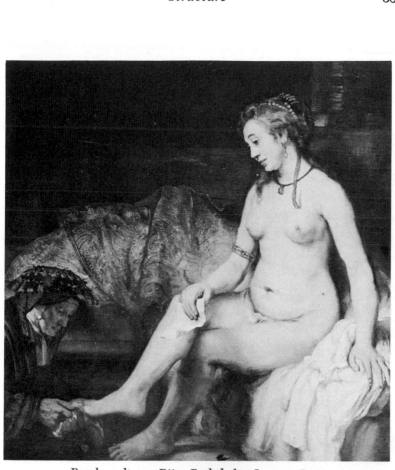

Rembrandt van Rijn, *Bathsheba. Louvre, Paris*

It is never easy to judge a work of art. Some may believe that good judgment will automatically follow the cultivation of good taste, but judgment comes as slowly and mysteriously as creation itself.

In such matters of taste, even a classicist such as Ingres sometimes succumbed to the romantic sentimentality of his time. In his *Francesca and Paolo,* a young man is proposing to a seated young woman who, overcome with emotion, has dropped her book; incredibly, the book remains suspended in midair. Here, Ingres yields to a nineteenth-century confusion that often equated histrionics with painting. Francesca dropping her book would produce a fine effect on the romantic stage, where playgoers were accustomed to the excesses of emotion; in the world of painting, however, this gesture introduces a ridiculous element. This painting illustrates a subjective lapse of taste in the early career of one of the last century's great painters.

In W. Holman Hunt's *The Awakened Conscience,* on the other hand, the sentimentality of the structure is as offensive as the idea expressed. It is impossible to read the picture visually. For example, the lower part of the woman's skirt might well be a lap blanket; and the seated man seems to have no legs. There is nothing in the painting to indicate that he has.

The elegant boulevardier in Manet's portraits, the refinement of his personages are so because of the elegance and refinement of Manet's temperament.

J. D. Ingres, *Francesca and Paolo. Ingres Museum, Angers*

W. Holman Hunt, *The Awakened Conscience. By permission of the Trustees of Sir Colin and Lady Anderson*

Édouard Manet, *In the Conservatory. Staatliche Museen Preussischer Kulturbesitz, Nationalgalerie, Berlin*

THE MYSTERY OF STRUCTURE

Henry James commented upon the "sacred mystery of structure," yet there are personalities of considerable ability who never penetrated this mystery and whose natures condemned them to leave but fragments of their imaginations. A criterion for an integrated structure is that an artist adhere faithfully to his chosen field of expression. Therefore painting is painting; sculpture is sculpture; music is not drama in a theatrical sense; literature is not the telling of a tale, but a complete development penetrating beyond the contours of personality, social life, and everyday events—often making sense out of an impossible premise. The art form transcends life in all its aspects, making Malraux's famous dialogue between the artist and the gods possible—a contest that would be one-sided in life and doom the human protagonist to defeat. One can sense this in the novels of Dostoevski and Kafka.

Stravinsky, writing of Berlioz and Wagner, referred to them as meteors fallen on an alien landscape. In Stravinsky's opinion, both of these composers encroached too deeply into the provinces of other art forms. Perhaps it would be best if we considered these "outsiders," as Goethe did the great poets, neither intellectuals nor artists, but as genius manifested beyond the scope of judgment.

Among these men of uneven genius, there is Michelangelo. Despite the imbalance between his art and his brooding cosmological aspirations, he attained an inner purity in his ultimate artistic development as painter, sculptor, and, above all, architect. His last works—the supposedly incomplete sculptures, *The Calling of Peter* (a fresco), and the magnificent design for the Laurentian Library in Florence—eloquently testify to this evolution. On the other hand, Rembrandt followed a consistent development from his early works to that period where his every brushstroke supports the fertile conception of a painter whose apparently simple works are really complex, reflecting strong, inventive structure. Rembrandt paints a beggar and the subject is a beggar. He can place a turban on the same poor man and paint him as a king, yet somehow we know the beggar is a king and the king is a beggar. Rembrandt's girl with a flower (we know her to be a milkmaid) is an Olympian goddess at the same time. In Rembrandt's dark-light world it is not gloom but richness and mystery that prevail.

Manoah's Offering, at the Dresden Museum, was painted during 1641. Some fourteen years later Rembrandt did a drawing of the same subject; it offers a splendid example of his creative evolution. The painting, typical of Rembrandt's virtuoso style of the 1640's, is somewhat theatrical in its intention and effect. The figures of Manoah and his wife (the parents of Samson) appear as if in the center of a stage, and the ghostlike angel ascending to Heaven in the upper left-hand corner, immediately above the sacrificial fire, appears like an ectoplasmic apparition in a spiritualistic seance.

In the drawing, however, Rembrandt's arrangement is such that the total event can be apprehended at a glance. There is none of the theatricality we find in the painting. The angel, for example, is to be imagined in the shape of the smoke as it rises from the burning offering, and the principal figures are completely joined in the powerful movement of the abstract interlocking forms.

We know that Rembrandt had great knowledge of composition at the time he painted the oil of this subject, but he nevertheless appears unsure in the integration of the entire work. On the other hand, Rembrandt began the drawing by placing the great movements, after which he apparently allowed the details to find a placement within these movements; in the painting, he must have begun with the placement of the objects and then found connections between them as best he could.

Although the images in the drawing are not as detailed as they are in the painting, they are not diminished—actually, they are all the more powerful because of the underlying

Rembrandt van Rijn, *Manoah's Offering. Staatliche Kunstsammlungen, Dresden*

Rembrandt van Rijn, *Manoah's Offering*. This drawing was made fourteen years after the original painting. *Collection Oskar Reinhart am Römerholz, Winterthur, Switzerland*

structure supporting them. We see that Rembrandt had gone from one truth to a greater one—an artistic truth, not a factual one.

In the paintings of Rembrandt, as with such painters as Cézanne, Titian, and Zurbarán, there is a structure relatively easy to define. Conversely, there is also a hidden structure impossible to analyze completely because it is so unbelievably mobile and represents the painter's personal concept. No one can fix the exact number of movements necessary to complete a drawing or painting, but when a complete balance has been attained, the movements appear to proliferate and indicate others that are not immediately apparent. It is not difficult to move free rhythms across a painting; it is difficult to give them distinction.

Formerly, when part of the training of a painter involved a period of copying the works of the masters, painters always remarked how much more they saw in Rembrandt's paintings as the copying progressed. In fact, Max Liebermann, the German Impressionist, remarked that seeing Rubens' paintings made him want to paint, while seeing Rembrandt's work made him want to give up painting.

OPTICS

Structure, which includes all of what we call composition, is based on the phenomenon of optics. If we all had one eye in the middle of our forehead, or two eyes placed one above the other, our whole orientation toward art would have developed in quite a different manner. In an optical sense, all works of art not only enliven the vision of the observer, but at the same time bring tranquillity to his sensibilities.

Interestingly, much of the search for a proper scale for paintings is conditioned by the fact that they rarely involve one's peripheral vision; the observer usually concentrates on the entire work from a fixed point. There are exceptions to this, of course, as in some of the huge baroque canvases such as Tintoretto's *Day of Judgment* and Veronese's monumental work at the Louvre, *The Nuptials at Cana,* where the observer is so surrounded by pictorial images that he must "read" them by moving from section to section. When such huge surfaces became the concern of the masters of the baroque style, the illusionistic art of the stage designer was even called into auxiliary service; and Tiepolo, that great Venetian baroque and rococo master, actually employed a stage designer named Colonna, who was his specialist for draperies and architectural perspectives.

If a person goes back far enough to encompass the entire surface of such large paintings, only the predominant rhythms will be revealed—certainly very little detail. With most sculpture, the viewer must actually walk around the work to see the whole; but as he does so, at each point of view he of course sees but one aspect of the entire work and accordingly must retain in memory his previous impressions.

SIMPLICITY

Though some sort of unity can be gained from confusion, such unity is rarely felicitous. Mathematicians, in speaking of several possible solutions to a given problem, invariably state that they prefer the more "elegant" solution—that is, the one that is most direct and simple.

Real directness and simplicity, of course, are not easily arrived at.

Brancusi, in speaking of some of the problems of the modern artist, said that simplicity was not the original aim of the artist, but a result of a great understanding of his craft. The young painter, then, even if he is not concerned with problems of representation, can certainly enrich his art and understanding by a penetrating study of the old masters and their archaic predecessors. It is not enough to read about the artists of the past in art histories that for the most part concern themselves with romantic storytelling episodes of an artist's life; actually, one must study these artists on their terms—in terms of the works they made.

In undertaking such a study, the student need not be confused by the variety of styles throughout the ages. These differences are essentially due to factors quite apart from basic pictorial structure. All the celebrated painters submitted themselves to the discipline of the four corners of the painted surface, and in doing so, have devised common strategies for overcoming that problem. While the interpretation of a painter like Rubens differs markedly from that of Giotto—one would be startled, for instance, to find the face of one of Rubens' Amazons on a Saint by Giotto—both of these painters shared a regard for an authoritative structure. The astute observer will find that underlying the sophisticated baroque rhythms and whirling arabesques of Rubens is the same gridwork of horizontal and vertical structure found in the early Renaissance masters. Were this not so, the very opulence of Rubens' style would make it impossible to read the painting.

Rubens is a painter difficult to identify since his own work and that of his studio assistants, such as Snyders and Van Dyck, are so joined in our minds. We must assume, however, that Rubens designed, or made the first sketches for the works that came from his studio. Sometimes, in the flamboyant and overbearing swirls and rhythms of works like the series of murals known as the Medici cycle, we assume that the major part of the execution was done by the assistants. In this painting, one of Rubens' best works, the fleshiness and exuberance of the forms are tempered by the great geometric shapes in which they exist, and the extension of which passes through the figures. It is this structure that makes Rubens' best work readable, despite the effulgence of the figural shapes. The volume and the activity in this painting are not centered, nevertheless they are discreetly removed from the sides. And the truths of natural observation are beautifully wedded to the truths and limitations of the picture plane.

Peter Paul Rubens, *Diana with the Nymphs and Satyrs. Staatliche Museen, Berlin*

Note the great geometric shapes in which the forms of this Rubens exist.

PLASTICITY AND "FREEDOM"

In this century, particularly, the plastic and physical aspects of painting have often been regarded as its sole aims, but to find an end in the plastic means alone would reduce painting to mere decoration. The painter does not simply paint pictures; he paints his relationship to something, his revelation of the world. Even though the nonobjectivist school holds that only the destruction of the object will free expression, freedom of expression will be attained—as always—from a change in concept toward the object.

A particular group of modern thinkers, some of whose concepts were expressed in art by the Constructivists and neo-Plasticists, felt that while art has served man throughout the ages, there remained but one more service it could render—to free man and to end art. The idea was drastically to change man's visual environment so that he would live surrounded by congenial color and perfectly functional, decorative buildings. The design of everything that affected man's life would be of such exquisite shapes as are mentioned by Plato in his "Syllabus." Within this suitable and agreeable environment, man, it was felt, would have no need, or purpose, to produce art since his very environment would fulfill that purpose. The unbearable burden of subjectivity and the malaise of fantasy were to be forever banished from the consciousness of suffering humanity. This curious marriage of romanticism and dialectic materialism—part of the concept of that brave new world formulated during the 1920's and 1930's—is now being revived, despite the flagrant error of this eschatology: such finality is both arrogant and ill-conceived.

THE GREAT STRUCTURAL ELEMENTS

Among the many structural techniques that can be profitably studied, four are outstanding. They are the integral tools of every competent painter. These technical devices concern the painter's visual responses to the world around him, as well as his thoughts and sentiments; they should always offer a means of achieving a far greater end than pictorial organization alone.

The four great structural elements are:

> Repetition
> Tempering of Volumes
> Tension
> Overlapping of Planes

All these elements may be observed in the painting by Duccio, *The Marys at the Sepulchre.*

Note the repetition in the shape of the rocks. But the lines we derive from the painting in the accompanying diagram are the main lines of rhythmic organization. They are set in opposition: vertically, diagonally, and horizontally. These lines tend to circumscribe the motif, giving the work stability and emphasis.

The tempering of volume brought out in the flat halo, behind the more voluminous head and torso of the angel, reminds us of the essential flatness of the surface. The horizontal fold of the angel's garment at the waist further modifies the volume of the figure as it joins the horizontal line of the sepulchre in that division of the total space.

The tension in a work of art is produced by opposition, the scale of different areas, as well as by directional movements and countermovements. The more powerful the opposition (this includes the opposition of color) the firmer will be the equilibrium of the work. Unlike balance, equilibrium is the product of the proper use of opposition and contrast. Any work of art will, of necessity, be realized through a unification of all the plastic forces; otherwise the work is only an arrangement of decorative motifs. The big tension in this Duccio, as demonstrated in the diagram, is also evidenced by the three-to-one relationship of the heads—that is, the three halos of the women, monotonous in their cadence, to the one isolated head of the angel.

Duccio. *The Marys at the Sepulchre. Opera del Duomo, Siena*

Repetition

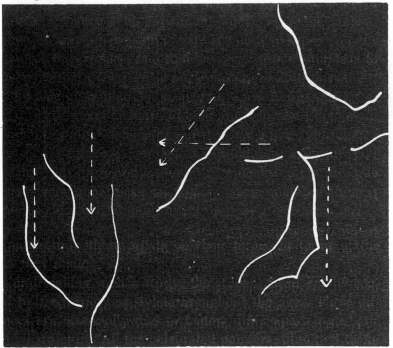

Tempering of volume

Tension

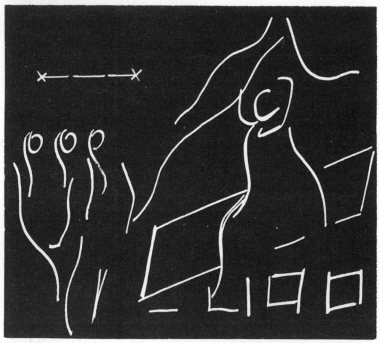

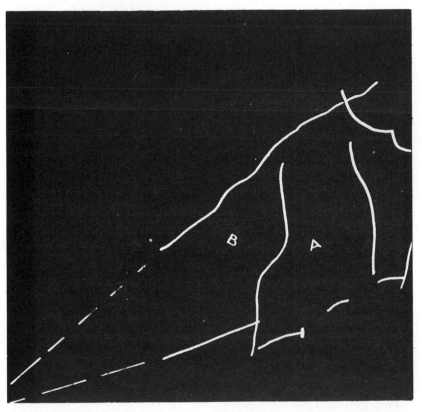

Overlapping of planes

In the above diagram, note how planes A and B overlap. In
their disposition, plane A projects the figure of the angel over
the background, plane B. Here the dual dimension of the picture is respected, without recourse to the illusion of mechanical
perspective or the convention of light and shadow.

An altarpiece by Cimabue.

Overlapping of planes in the Cima-bue altarpiece.

The overlapping of planes may also be seen in this diagram from an altarpiece by Cimabue. Note how in section A of the diagram the planes of the surface overlap and join the figure. The enormous movement in section B, from the center of the figure and down through the lap, has the character of a wing; this emphasizes the religious thought, as well as the aesthetic structure of the picture. This movement serves to unify the background and foreground. The smaller planes at the top also suggest wings; they culminate in the little angels—winged, of course.

The Resurrection, a fresco by Giotto. *Museo Civico, Padua*

REPETITION OF SHAPE

In Giotto's fresco the repetition of pear shapes not only provides the design, but affords the very rhythm emphasizing these forms. The shapes are, in turn, figure contours and area outlines. A distinct fringelike accent is repeated in the angel's wings, in Christ's feet, and in the hands and feet of the kneeling foreground figure. The circular halo repetition is obvious; what is interesting here is the spacing. From center to right, the three halos form a triangle. Each halo itself is the culminating point of a movement.

Repetition of an Oval Movement

This Bronzino, *Eleanora of Toledo and Her Son Don Garcia*, offers a good illustration of the repetition of ovals. In the faces of the woman and the little boy the ovals suggest volume, while in the body of the boy the oval form is a rich, two-dimensional design movement. As it falls over the woman's bosom, the oval necklace suggests three dimensions, but to a shallower degree than is evidenced in the face. The large oval arc, in the center of the figure, negates the cylindrical volume of the torso.

Bronzino, *Eleanora of Toledo and Her Son Don Garcia. Uffizi, Florence*

Note the repetition of the oval movement in this diagram from Bronzino's
Eleanora of Toledo.

Note the tempering of volumes in this diagram.

The two oval arcs at the bottom of the picture are thrusts, the center one against the movement of the woman's left arm. The two lower arcs form the base of a tower of ovals encompassing the large central arc, the necklace, and culminating in the head. The face is enclosed within a large oval, the axis of which forms a pyramid, ending at the line where the brow meets the hair. The boy's head is a small oval jutting above that describing his body; in essence, this is the simple structure of a snow-man.

TEMPERING OF VOLUMES

One is impressed by a feeling of completion and fullness upon viewing this painting of Bronzino. This late-Renaissance master, often referred to as a Mannerist, managed his volumes in a very discreet and logical way. One of the most obvious techniques is the manner in which all the curved movements are tempered by diagonal, horizontal, or vertical directions on the canvas. Horizontal and vertical divisions of the rectangle are also employed to achieve a proper unity between the empty background and the two figures. The curves in the painting are noticeably fuller toward the center, and are shallower as they approach the extremities of the picture. For instance, the little boy's face is much rounder on the side near his mother, while the other side of his face almost parallels the edge of the can-vas. On the dress, encompassing the left arm of the lady, the curves in the ruffles billow in the inner part. They are straighter, or more rhomboid in character, toward the left boundary of the painting. The curving movement of the left arm tends to be straight from the elbow to the little finger of the left hand. The flat areas of the painting encompass the shapes of the figures (as is indicated by the dotted lines) through the movement of beautifully proportioned planes.

In Rubens' painting *The Three Graces*, the greater volumi-nous emphasis on the center figure, as contrasted to the figures on the left and right, is achieved through a greater overlay of planes.

Peter Paul Rubens, *The Three Graces. Museo del Prado, Madrid*

Picasso's painting *Three Musicians,* on the other hand, has far fewer curvilinear shapes than the Rubens; nevertheless, there is the same overlay of planes at the center of the composition that we observed in *The Three Graces.*

The concentration of volumes within the center areas of a painting is a classical device but it is not the only way of achieving a sense of fullness in a picture. A similar effect can be obtained through equilibrated horizontal, vertical, and diagonal movements that culminate in a manner sufficient to give an actual or an implied feeling of fullness. Often in paintings where the representational elements are inconspicuous, and even eliminated, the sense of fullness is obtained by the impact of a variety of plastic elements at the point where these elements converge, for instance, in a Chinese classical landscape the point where a hill, or a bamboo stalk, becomes one with the rest of the surface. This optical phenomenon is based on the action of heterogeneous elements working against simpler elements—of straight lines opposite those that are curved.

In *The Fisherman* by Chang Lu, we observe this kind of action in the play of the small boat and the boatman's pole against the large rock; it is also present in the contrast of the leaves, which appear almost as the wings of small birds, to the rock and the boulder at the bottom of the painting. Finally, it is also evident in the marvelous relations between the large empty areas and the perfectly placed tactile accents.

ILLUSIONISM

The physical reality of the pictorial surface allows for only these two dimensions, the vertical and the horizontal. Therefore, whether an artist's objective is to render the objects, or the spaces, of the perceived world, this objective can be achieved only by illusionism.

In the development of a painting, the grouping of the forms to give this illusion of volume need not be centered, as it is with Rubens' *The Three Graces.* In time, it became a conven-

Pablo Picasso, *Three Musicians. Collection, Museum of Modern Art, New York. Mrs. Simon Guggenheim Fund*

Chang Lu, *The Fish-
erman. Courtesy M.
Yemori, Tokyo*

tion of Western painting to place the most interesting and voluminous parts in the center of the picture, but with Chang Lu's work, it is not the main figure of the fisherman that one would ordinarily expect to be projected; actually it is the negative area above the horizontal of the boat. This is accomplished by the backward thrust of the lower part of the painting and the impact of the diagonal from the lower right edge of the rock along the pole, which separates the right side of the painting from the lower left.

Another sort of optical illusion that the painter must be most concerned with is the backward tilting of the painting as the artist begins to work on an empty canvas. If we stand before a fairly large blank wall we most often assume, thoughtlessly, that our line of vision is equidistant from all the sections of the wall. In retrospect we know this to be untrue. Now, since we regard the canvas more as a wall than a window, it is necessary to make allowances for our distortions in vision. This factor in our vision has long been recognized, especially among painters of large pictures, where violent activity is involved. In Michelangelo's frescoes in the Sistine Chapel of *The Day of Judgment*, for instance, the two main groupings of figures, to the left and right, are so agitated in movement that Michelangelo, when he supervised the construction of the wall, ordered a forward tilt of some forty-four inches at the topmost section. As a matter of procedure, the full upper sections of the painting should be projected in order to compensate for the backward tilt of the picture plane as shown in the accompanying diagram.

In the famous late painting of Mont Sainte-Victoire by Cézanne, the upper two-thirds of the painting is projected by means of an array of horizontals in the lower sections of the painting. These horizontal movements are discernible in the foliage of the trees and at the bottom of the mountain. Thus the verticality of the painting is reestablished and, despite the perspective, the mountain and the sky of the distance exist in a frontal plane.

IDEAS AND STRUCTURE

To avoid mere decorative statement, artistic structure should actually encompass the ideas a painter wishes to express. Of course, since the ideas of painters are constantly changing, there comes a point when something is lacking in the structural possibilities of all styles. This deficiency is not necessarily inherent in the original concept; but it becomes necessary to make a departure when new experience demands more than a given concept allows.

The need for firm design in Impressionist painting became evident after the new approach to color and the casualness of the original version had been attained. This was the aim and purpose of the neo-Impressionists Seurat and Signac, and of Degas. However, we should remember that Impressionist painters introduced the Japanese silhouette into Western painting.

Matisse, who desired the effect created by large areas of sonorous color, kept these areas relatively simple. Had these areas been too complex, they would have vitiated the power of the color. Incidentally, Matisse criticized the spot structure of the neo-Impressionists as lacking drama. Since he had once employed neo-Impressionist methods, he was well able to criticize this style, in which he said one moved tentatively from spot to spot, gradually arriving at an outline. In contrast to Matisse's method, when a richness of graphic detail and contour is sought, as in a painting by Van Eyck or Dürer, the color is usually considered with discretion, often being controlled by a tonality.

PICTORIAL STATEMENT

Late in the nineteenth century, when Cézanne applied his knowledge of Venetian painting in seeking a more stable composition, he avoided any attempt to revive baroque painting.

And in the century after Giotto, Jacopo Bellini, Mantegna, Masaccio, Signorelli, and Uccello explored new vistas of isometric drawing and perspective in acquiring the experience that culminated in the High Renaissance. Effective structure coincides with a painter's purpose, the end he has in mind for the pictorial statement of his ideas. When Cézanne used the spiraling movement he had observed in baroque painting, his purpose was to interrelate the many spots of color on his canvas, as in his late painting of the gardener Vallier.

Cézanne's hegira from the point of his early works like the *Olympia* and *The Portrait of Achille L'Empéraire*, and even such a middle-period landscape as *The Turn in the Road*, to that

Paul Cézanne, *The Turn in the Road. Courtesy, Museum of Fine Arts, Boston. Bequest of John T. Spaulding*

Mecca of the sensibilities he reached in *The Portrait of the Gardener Vallier* was both long and difficult. He first had to absorb the pictorial experience of the carefully planned still lifes and landscapes of his middle period. At this point in his artistic journeying, he owed much to his friend Pissarro in whose company he painted landscapes around Pontoise and Auvers-sur-Oise over the two-year period 1872 to 1874. After this association, there was an evident structural improvement in Cézanne's work.

Today, in a period, as Bertrand Russell once said, when events that previously had taken a century to develop are compressed into a decade, there exists the pitfall of attempting to equate today's concept with yesterday's structural means. It is difficult for a painter to express himself verbally in matters of visual perception, though he can record his analytical studies. No real artist paints a picture or does a sculpture to reveal the construction of the work; he does so to create an image. André Derain, convinced that Cubism revealed too much of the means employed, actually cautioned that it was necessary to hide the construction of a painting.

For the student-artist or the artist-student, it is often helpful to sublimate admiration for a work of art in order to study more carefully the pictorial design. Some years ago when one of the authors was working in Munich, it was difficult for Americans to find pants cut in the manner to which they were accustomed. Finally, a tailor asked one of the Americans to give him a pair of American-made pants, so that he could study their construction. This was done, the pants were duly "dissected," and thereafter the tailor made pants for most of the American students. He had discovered an essential of American tailoring that was previously hidden from him.

The most profitable study of pictorial structure is best undertaken dispassionately, without thought toward immediate use in one's work. In such a study, no laws will be found to be always applicable. Discovery of the individual principles of structure and an awareness of artistic style should be one's objectives.

Accordingly, we have undertaken a series of studies, beginning with a detailed analysis of the Unicorn Tapestry since the concept and the means employed in this work have been resolved in such perfect harmony. What calm and constant elevation must have been in the spirit of the master designer of these tapestries. If only on the basis of the patience required for its completion, the contemporary artist is incapable of such involved design; as Paul Valéry observed, man's patience was destroyed by the machine. Yet we must not forget that the form content on which this work is based is not the pure invention of its creator. This is one of those complete works of art that, like Grünewald's *Isenheim Altar* and Raphael's *Borgia Suite,* are the culminating efforts of a strong tradition.

THE HUNT OF THE UNICORN

Like the notes to the prelude of a fugue, the elements of this design appear in measured rhythm. All but one of the dogs have at least three legs on the ground. The hunter's legs are slender triangles, spread no farther apart than the prongs of a hairpin. A simple diamond shape, up-ended, contains the hunters and the dogs. Throughout the composition a narrow V-shaped form is evidenced. Vertical and horizontal elements of the design are emphasized to stabilize the composition. For the same reason, the dogs' tails and the hunters' plumed hat are conceived as shallow curves, almost equal in degree. The hunter who stands in the center of the panel divides it vertically; this central division is maintained, with mild variations, throughout the series. There is more rhythmic movement on the right side of the panel, leading to the second tapestry, where the unicorn will be introduced.

In the second panel, we meet the unicorn, his horn immersed in the stream that parallels the base of the tapestry. Above the unicorn is a fountain; the column of the fountain forms the central division of this panel. The hunters are arranged in an arc about the fountain-bowl; this arc-like movement repeats that of the fountain-bowl. Toward the top of the panel, trees form a horizontal band, repeating the line of the stream.

Note how the unicorn is surrounded. His tail, buttocks, and neck, almost horizontal in character, add to the illusion of the animal's confinement. Everything in the shapes and in the disposition of the forms accentuates this encirclement.

Enchanting animals gaze upward, indifferent to the drama, while the animal shapes are more active than the figural parts. The diamond shape, containing the unicorn and the hunters, is wider than it is high.

In the third tapestry, the unicorn attempts to escape. Just below the stream, flowing now from top to bottom, a tree divides the panel vertically. The unicorn, his haunches immersed in the water, is a lunging shape; his burst for freedom is well depicted. His forelegs drop from the knee, suggesting a barrier further supported by the vertical horn strap and scabbard of the hunter ahead. The aim of the hunters' spears virtually fixes the unicorn as a wheel hub hemmed in by spokes. Ironically, one of these spears is not a spear at all but the unicorn's own horn. The cadent arrangement of the hunters' spears at the top of the panel further evokes the captive theme.

In the fourth panel, the unicorn defends himself. To keep the animal from getting away, the hunters shift to the right side of the panel. Again, a tree serves as the vertical divider. Only the unicorn's bucking hindquarters connect with the left side of the tapestry; this limits his maneuvering ground considerably. In the preceding panel, the hunters were dispersed into small, asymmetrical, triangle-patterned groups. This lent agitation to the composition. Here, however, the straight angle of the hunter's spear, directly behind the unicorn, divides the panel horizontally. Beyond the thrusting hunter, a sense of tranquillity pervades the left periphery. Two leaping dogs, practically identical, lend a near-monotony that tends to pacify the lower section.

The drama centers at the right. The unicorn, two of the dogs, and the cap of the grim-faced hunter comprise the lightest areas in the right section, areas that are beautifully related. The unicorn prods a dog—the only instance where the animals come to grips with one another—and the gored dog acts as this panel's barrier to the unicorn's escape.

In the upper left-hand corner of the sixth panel, the unicorn is wounded by the spear thrusts. There is an interesting time sequence here, for at the center of the panel the unicorn is depicted slain and slung ingloriously over the back of a horse. The animal's right foreleg, buckled, forms an angle that isolates the left corner section from the rest of the panel; this was a traditional means of portraying the passage of time in composition. The generously curved forms of the castle folk, the reposing postures of the hunters and dogs, and the stabilizing verticals and horizontals all indicate that the excitement of the hunt is over; the fugue is resolved.

The figures of the courtiers are poised on the picture plane like a suspended drop of oil. As they point toward the center of the panel, the spears of the hunters are in a less angular arrangement than before. The chief hunter, alongside the horse, and the tree above him form the dividing vertical of this tapestry.

In the last panel, the unicorn is again shown alive and content, confined to a wooden enclosure surrounded by a paradisiacal setting of flower and fern. His horn blends with the trunk of a tree in the center and forms part of an inverted V.

The hunt has been interpreted as being symbolic of the Christ story. To support this interpretation, several of the dogs have IHS emblazoned on their collars; the maiden in the fifth tapestry (not shown, because only fragments of the original remain) is a symbol of the mother of Christ; and the unicorn who is hunted, speared, and finally restored to life is the Christ. It is apparent then, why, in the last panel, the resurrected unicorn lives in a circular enclosure that resembles a crown.

The Hunt of the Unicorn, often called *The Unicorn Tapestry,* was made in the late fifteenth century of wool and silk with silver and silver-gilt threads. *All photos in this series: The Metropolitan Museum of Art, The Cloisters Collection. Gift of John D. Rockefeller, Jr., 1937*

I   The Start of the Hunt

II   The Unicorn at the Fountain

III   The Unicorn Tries to Escape

IV   The Unicorn Defends Himself

VI   The Unicorn Is Brought to the Castle

VII   The Unicorn in Captivity

USES OF THE PAST

Pictorial structure, in part, rests on the arrangement of related shapes; these relationships can be studied. Samuel Butler makes this comment in his *Journal:* "A man must command all the resources of his art and of these none is greater than knowledge of what has been done by predecessors. What, I wonder, can he take from these—how may he build himself upon them and grow out of them—if he is to make it his chief business to steer clear of them?" And André Gide, who acknowledged the personal vision of the artist, said that this did not mean most original talents are uncultivated.

It is in matters of composition, especially, that the greatest painters studied their predecessors for solutions of their own problems. One of the reasons this study of the past has been disputed in recent years is the exaggerated confidence we inherited from the nineteenth century in using nature as a source of study. The nineteenth-century man had a confidence in nature that we have in technology today. Also, academic study in the past century had become dull, uninspired copy work, and the painters were concerned with many facets that now seem extraneous to us.

We hope to clarify this point further by examining two paintings by Manet and Picasso that appear to have been inspired by older works of art. In addition, we shall compare a painting of Rubens that was certainly inspired by one of Caravaggio's works.

GOYA AND MANET

There is a distinct relationship between Manet's *Execution of the Emperor Maximilian of Mexico* and Goya's *The Execution of the Rebels on May 3rd, 1808*, or, as it is commonly known, *The Massacre*—a relationship that extends even beyond a similar technical means. The theme of Napoleonic soldiers executing Spanish patriots is imaginatively exploited in the

Édouard Manet, *The Execution of the Emperor Maximilian of Mexico. Städtische Kunsthalle, Mannheim*

Goya, *The Execution of the Rebels on May 3rd, 1808 (The Massacre). Museo del Prado, Madrid*

canvas by Goya; in Manet's painting the soldiers, who are part
Spanish in descent, are executing a usurper of the Mexican
throne—a man who had been given his throne by another
Napoleon. Artists can be inspired by an image of the mind as
well as by works of other artists. In Manet's case, he did not
witness the execution of Maximilian; the event came to his
attention through accounts in periodicals. In completing the
painting, Manet did not imitate the exact form of Goya; had
Manet been a musician, the work might have been classified
as *Variations on a Theme by Goya.*

The canvases of Goya and Manet have almost similar proportions. The figures in both compositions form bands across
the surface beginning about an eighth of the distance from the
bottom to the top. The firing squads in both works are on
nearly the same horizontal line. A linear movement runs diagonally through the line of the hill at the upper left of *The
Massacre,* culminating in the guns. In the Manet, there is no
hill, but the top of the wall is comparable to the horizontal in
the Goya where the rooftops meet the sides of the building in
the background. The outline of these rooftops is rhythmically
similar to the foliage above the garden wall in the Manet. The
figural gestures painted by Goya, who did not have a purely
objective attitude toward war and its resultant cruelty, are
highly dramatic. In fact, it is remarkable that Goya could have
expressed his emotions with such formal distinction, yet had
he observed with only the eye of a patriot and humanist his
work would hold little interest for us today.

Observe how the soldiers in Goya's work are bent forward
to form increasingly acute angles. Their helmets rest on a gen-
erous curve and they tilt in an arresting cadence of movement.
The group of victims are a solid mass circumscribed above by
a curve that begins with the arms of the figure in the white
shirt, on the extreme right. The left arm of the same man, pointing upward, is compositionally similar to the left contour of the
puff of smoke in Manet's painting.

In both works, the two groupings of the victims and executioners are structurally circumscribed by curves of a similar nature. There is a diagonal line dogging the lower left side of both pictures. In *The Massacre,* it is a sharp line marking the division of light thrown by the lamp and passing upward through the first soldier; Manet indicated a corresponding diagonal by means of a shadow thrown by the soldier in the center of the picture. This diagonal movement passes through the rifle of the soldier reloading his piece, then moves out of the right side of the canvas.

Between the two groupings, in both paintings, there is an intermediate figure just left of the central division. In the Goya, it is the figure who covers his eyes with his hands; in the Manet, the first soldier in the firing squad. There are sharp, slicing diagonals on the left side of both pictures. In *The Massacre* it is sharp and leads down the left arm of the white-shirted figure to the patriot who lies sprawled in his own blood. We can trace a like diagonal in the Manet through the trouser leg of the victim on the far left, as he falls back from the bullets' impact.

Despite these similarities, however, there are also essential differences between the compositions. *The Massacre,* with its diagonal movements and sweeping curves, is dynamic in character; Manet's rectangular forms render a more static composition. While the Goya is agitated, the Manet is emotionally restrained. Goya's victims writhe and twist as they wait to be shot; the Emperor Maximilian and his followers stand stiff-legged. Goya's soldiers stand well forward; Manet's assume a more casual stance.

Manet's work, which is more scientifically objective, was done some sixty years after Goya's romantically inspired work. Although he did have an anti-Napoleonic bias (there is a curious resemblance between the man on Maximilian's left and Napoleon III), Manet was not a revolutionary spirit either in the social or political sense: his life poses the same contradiction as Cézanne's—two artists of conservative character whose works were nevertheless of such a zealous nature that we are still inspired by their impact.

PICASSO AND A SPANISH ROMANESQUE PLAQUE

While today's artist is generally interested only in acquiring the technical facility necessary to express his personality, it must be admitted that an artist's preference for certain epochs implies an emotional affinity for those particular periods of the past. Miró remains close in his interest to the Spanish tradition,

Pablo Picasso, *The Sailor. Courtesy Samuel Kootz Gallery, New York*

while Picasso and Matisse, who both made adaptations of other works, usually remain faithful to the space and volume dispositions of the original works.

In noting the resemblance between the Romanesque plaque and Picasso's portrait, we must not exclude the fact that Picasso may have been inspired by two realities. The Romanesque plaque he may have studied might have been as real an inspiration as the person who sat for the portrait. Since inspiration is a complex matter it is rare that an immediate experi-

Joseph, from an Adoration Group—a Romanesque plaque. *The Metropolitan Museum of Art, The Cloisters Collection, 1930*

ence will be the sole source of inspiration for a work of art. In fact, an immediate experience is without value unless the essence of that experience has not already germinated within the artist's mind.

Note the resemblance between this Spanish Romanesque plaque and Picasso's portrait of a sailor. (Although our comparison is conscious, Picasso's inspiration may have lain elsewhere—since there is always the possibility of coincidence.) The portrait of the sailor is a three-quarter-length seated figure, while in the Romanesque plaque the figure is full length. The character of the plaque is concentrated in the upper half—in the turning of the saint's trunk and in the tilt of the head resting on the fist. The resemblance is noticeable in three important aspects: the unusual pose; the volume relations of head, arm, and trunk; and the arrangement of areas, including the spotting of circles. In the plaque, these circular arrangements occur in the stylization of the knees, the left shoulder, and the right elbow; in the Picasso, the chair knobs, the wrist of the hand supporting the head, and the circle under the left hand. Both compositions are split by a central division. This is observed in the plaque by following a curve that begins at the ear, rises upward past the left eyebrow, and then continues downward past the right eyebrow, the right hand, and the supporting arm. In the same manner as in the plaque, the curve begins at the sailor's left ear and rises upward past the left eyebrow and descends in a line comparable to the outer edge of the saint's garment. The sailor's left arm, with the hand resting on the knee, is similar in construction to that of the saint. The hands of both their right arms are supported on a full circle. The lines on the sailor's blouse rather approximate the folds of the saint's cloak.

Though there are other similarities, it is pertinent here to indicate the differences in the two works. In our opinion, Picasso's painting is richer in design, invention, and imagery.

Even though both figures fill out most of the surface area, Picasso's subtle manipulations have taken his figure off the straight vertical axis of the rectangle. This is apparent in the shift of the head and the several planing movements that pass in opposing directions through the head. By the constant employment of such activity throughout the painting, Picasso has managed more surface tension, so that his sailor seems far more dynamic than St. Joseph.

CARAVAGGIO AND RUBENS

Like Picasso today, Peter Paul Rubens was a painter of great scholarship. As a young man he spent eight years in Italy where he made many copies of Venetian paintings. But he also did other studies: a fine copy of the *Battle of Anghiari* (the now-lost work of Leonardo) as well as some of Michelangelo's works. In his copies, Rubens was faithful to the originals and did not attempt actual interpretations of the other painters, as Picasso and Van Gogh have done. Of course, in his copies the handwriting of Rubens was evident—for he was a forceful personality and an outstanding talent.

But in this obvious copy of Caravaggio's *Entombment of Christ,* Rubens did attempt to revise Caravaggio, trying to resolve the diffuse lighter areas into more pacific unity, this in fact he does, containing them in one rhythmic mass. Also, Rubens seemed concerned with maintaining a firmer frontal plane than did Caravaggio, whose painting has a greater movement into depth. Rubens reduced the oblique thrust of the stone slab and thereby maintained the frontal plane, minimizing the depth beneath. The extended hands of the mourners in the original are eliminated in the copy. It is possible that Rubens believed this aspect weakened the impact of the figures. Some of the dramatic light effects of Caravaggio also disappear.

We do not maintain that Rubens' copy is an improvement over the original, but it does show clearly an important con-

Caravaggio, *The Entombment of Christ. Vatican, Vatican City*

Peter Paul Rubens, *The Entombment of Christ. The National Gallery of Canada, Ottawa*

ceptual difference between the two great baroque painters, whose styles were adapted to the stress of continuous movement. To Rubens, the dramatic agitation of this Caravaggio did not advance the arabesque character of the style.

Though Rubens made pertinent alterations, there are elements in Caravaggio's painting that appear to be structurally more sound. For instance, there is a horizontal movement in the Caravaggio about a third of the way from the top; turning the illustration upside down will emphasize this movement. It moves across the back of the man holding the legs of Christ, on through this man's face, terminating in the thumb and forefinger of the hand directly above the Saviour. This horizontal, along with the one delineating the top of the slab, creates a rectangle on which much of the pictorial structure depends.

STRUCTURE AND THE INDIVIDUAL TALENT

It is ridiculous to imagine that a painter can approach a canvas with a slide rule and measure the correct proportions of beauty and truth, though to stand before the canvas confused and uninformed—with nothing more than a passionate desire to "make a realized work of art"—proves equally frustrating. Many artists have commented on the agonizing moments of their youth when they were consumed by the "divine fire" but were unable to realize the dreams in their minds.

With the painter, the supreme interpretation of pictorial structure lies in a change in his character and vision to a oneness with all the means of his medium, and with art itself. This change may not be a natural one: it calls a person to a more highly organized state of being.

Each painter has only one mind, one rhythm, and one kind of order with which to achieve a clear, persuasive structure.

A realized structure is exacting in its spiritual and intellectual demands, and it unites such complexities as a sense of the past, as well as the total response of the painter to his craft, to himself, and to the life about him.

III

Space

THE PAINTER'S
REALIZATION OF
SPACE

We see the visible world as an expanse of objects in space, but since we are unable to encompass all of space we must limit it. We build walls; we close doors: we feel secure only in that proportion of space suitable to us.

As a painter translates his impressions of the visible world onto canvas, he is dealing with a limited space. Yet within the relatively narrow dimensions of a canvas he can suggest vast landscapes; people in all manner of activity; the many textures of objects. In this section we shall describe some of the problems that painters have faced in trying to translate a three-dimensional world into a two-dimensional area—and some of the solutions they found. A painter faces this problem with his first stroke, and as the work progresses the many marks must be resolved, because the main characteristic as well as the aim of pictorial composition is unity.

SPACE AND THE HISTORICAL MOMENT

In part, we have limited space by our differing concepts of space throughout history. It would not be in the scope of this essay to treat of the many scientific and philosophical concepts of space; but these concepts, for the most part indirectly, have certainly influenced the painter.

For example, we can now comprehend some of the problems of journeying through outer space, and soon man will be landing on the moon. This will affect the way painters, in their particular time, translate their perceptions of space. Today, moments after a jet liner takes off, serene landscapes such as Hobbema and Ruisdael painted are seen as patchwork quilts. At the other extreme, the microscope has revealed that the perfect rectangle is not the creation of man alone, but exists within the minute facets of crystals. The driving force of certain minute organisms across a slide resembles the heavenly constellations as well as the improvised spots and dashes of some abstract Impressionist paintings, notably the early series of Kandinsky. The shrinking concept of the earth in which it is possible for a man on one side of the world to encounter another, on the opposite side, in a matter of hours, has inspired artists to enlarge their spatial visions, in spite of the fact that by now the phrase "cosmic space" has begun to grate on one's sensibilities.

Since men envision the world in many ways, they have concomitantly devised many spatial structures. Spatial structures are the architecture for describing the visible world. Long before there was a written language, cavemen depicted their interest in animals and hunting. In their landscapes, Chinese painters, especially of the great classical periods during the Tang, Ming, and Sung dynasties, expressed their whole philosophy of life by unifying man with the life-force of nature. But, in the sight of Apollo, the spatial concepts of the cavemen, the Chinese painters, the baroque masters, and many others, are equally valid. Spatial elegance has nothing to do with literalness, with correct perspective, or with an illusion of depth.

Obviously, medieval man could not have conceived space as we do; he lived within too narrow a world. Travel was difficult and dangerous; there were the confining and dogmatic tenets of religion and the feudal economy. Yet medieval painters needed only a shallow depth to project, in their many great works of art, the faith that sustained them in the restricted and often tragic dimensions of their world. In contrast, the deep perspectives of Tintoretto and Veronese, who painted in the seventeenth century when scientists, voyagers, and philosophers were exploring the world in fact and in thought, are pictorial evidence of the interest in an expanding world.

Oil paint is, after all, only a kind of colored grease, but when used by a fine painter it can create wondrous illusions. Thinly colored planes can suggest by their interaction the seemingly rounded figures of Veronese, the deep folds in a Zurbarán, the landscapes of a Ruisdael, and the subtleties of texture and surface in a Braque.

Georges Braque, *Man with a Guitar. Collection, The Museum of Modern Art, New York. Lillie P. Bliss Bequest*

◄ Jacob van Ruisdael, *Haarlem from the Dunes. Courtesy, Museum of Fine Arts, Boston*

Francisco de Zurbarán,
Saint Serapion. Courtesy,
The Wadsworth Atheneum,
Hartford

Paolo Veronese, *Mars and*
Venus United by Love.
The Metropolitan Museum
of Art, New York. Kennedy
Fund

Madonna and Child with Two Angels. Italo-Byzantine panel, thirteenth century. *The Currier Gallery of Art, Manchester, New Hampshire*

Tintoretto, *The Baptism of Christ. Scuola di San Rocco, Venice*

El Greco, Tintoretto, and Titian all followed the Venetian baroque tradition, yet each of these painters had a personal approach to space. Just as everyone has preferences and aversions, so do artists have their own feelings for form and space within a particular style.

With El Greco, an intensely religious man, we must reject standards that we usually apply to reality. In his paintings, even such inanimate objects as clouds and rocks shine in the same ecstasy as do saints and martyrs. The space of El Greco is slightly concave and shallower than Tintoretto's, but then El Greco's first influence in his native Crete was the icon. In these works, the space is conceived quite flat.

Tintoretto depicted a world brimming with gestures. Titian, as he matured, evolved a vibrating color space. His patches of broken color predate a method used by the Impressionists. Color on the contours of Titian's figures appears often dissolved in light, just as the sky, buildings, and water appear to blend together in the haze of the Venetian sun.

In the nineteenth century, along with the development of photography, spatial vision was largely inspired by the desire to represent the literal and to concentrate more and more on what the eye, and the eye alone, sees. Courbet, Monet, and Manet extended this vision to explore new vistas of form and color; on the other hand, the academicians confounded this vision, and despite their claims that they were carrying on the ideals of past ages, as Baudelaire said of them, they represented no tradition but their own.

No matter what spatial or stylistic device he employs, each painter must work on a picture surface that has only two dimensions: width and height. To accentuate the difference between actual and pictorial space, assume that the surface of a painting is the front side of a glass aquarium, the kind found in any pet store. The aquarium is filled with blue-green water. Swaying ferns, darting fish, and bubbles rising to the surface make all the relations approximate. If we look straight through the

Titian, *The Entombment. Museo del Prado, Madrid*

El Greco, *Saint Jerome. The Frick Collection, New York*

sides of the aquarium, we realize a sensation of infinity. But if a large fish or a rock is dropped into the tank, the previous relations are disturbed and we no longer have a feeling of infinite depth. Instead we have only the actual foot or so of depth.

A painter does not have this foot of depth in which to work. Instead, he has only a flat surface that he disturbs the moment he begins to paint on it, the same way the large rock, when it was dropped, qualified the relations in the aquarium.

MOVEMENT AND COUNTERMOVEMENT

Because of these factors, the painter must act decisively in controlling the various relations in his space. A strong diagonal movement through a painting can be balanced only by an

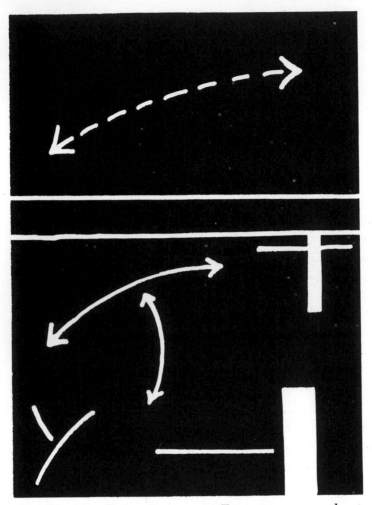

MOVEMENT AND COUNTERMOVEMENT. Every movement or thrust, whether into the surface or against it, must have a countermovement to establish an equilibrium. Note how in this diagram the two-headed arrow swings *away* from the surface.

Now study this demonstration of movement and countermovement. The white planes show the vertical movements while the thinner straight lines show the horizontal planes. The double-headed arrows indicate the curved movements and countermovements, as do the two lines about to cross each other in the lower left-hand corner.

action at right angles to it. Curves are resolved by counter-curves. A horizontal movement is set against a vertical as is seen in the work of Mondrian. Flat shapes are best adjusted in larger areas, as happens when the various appendages of the body are connected in a figural image. Unless compensating movements reaffirm the two-dimensional order of the plane, the effect is similar to that of a hole punched into the painting. The average observer, who might not be familiar with all the technical aspects of painting, nevertheless reacts to the blatant disorders of the picture surface in the same way he would sense a person's disordered mind—without being able to make a medical diagnosis.

SPATIAL RELATIONS

With maturity, each painter becomes more sensitive in his ability to see and develop these spatial relationships. Courbet was seated in a café one evening when a man, pointing to some dice on the table, asked him if he could paint them any better than an academic painter. Courbet answered that most academicians could paint the individual dice pieces as well as he could, "But what they can't do in their work," said Courbet, "is show the relationship between the various pieces."

Chardin and Cézanne were two painters who developed their visual judgment to accommodate an extraordinary sensitivity to the relations between objects. By means of Chardin's exquisite relations of space we perceive the roundness of the pitchers and what object is in front of another. We feel the distance from the tip of the ledge to the rear wall. This wall does not merely serve as a background, it is an integral part of the space, completely unified within the painting.

SPACE, ORDER, AND SCIENCE

This desire for relationship and order in space, as in life, is not merely a technical concern: it is part of a need within all of us. Each painter obeys this need in accordance with his

Jean-Baptiste Siméon Chardin, *Still Life: Kitchen Table. Courtesy, Museum of Fine Arts, Boston. Gift of Mrs. Peter Chardon Brooks*

Paul Cézanne, *The Card Players. The Metropolitan Museum of Art, New York. Bequest of Stephen C. Clark, 1960*

temperament. Some painters may prefer a geometrically justified unity, as did Mondrian, Poussin, and Seurat. Others may embrace an emotional or intuitive way of ordering their sensory and visual perceptions, as did Delacroix (who said, "feeling will do wonders"), Munch, and Van Gogh.

In painting, order is space and space is order. In an attempt to systemize space, some painters like Juan Gris, André Lhote, and Jacques Villon have sought aid from mathematics and the other sciences. Painters should accept whatever assistance they need, although it would seem that some things are better left to the scientists. One advantage painting offers is an approach toward self-disciplined freedom and a judgment of reality, other than that given by microscopes and computers. Yet some continually try to turn the painter into a complete scientist.

A number of recent articles have shown enlargements of microslides, aerial photographs, and biological specimens, citing their alleged similarity to nonobjective painting—all this, of course, long after the fact. Harold G. Cassidy, in his book *The Sciences and the Arts—A New Alliance*, prophetically warns artists of the fate awaiting them should they ignore the disciplines of science. "An artist," Mr. Cassidy writes, "is implicitly an interpreter of his age . . . assuredly if today's artists do not take the responsibility of understanding modern science and what it accomplishes and of applying their own unique gifts to interpreting it for the rest of us, they will destroy art—and themselves."

Since the Renaissance, this notion of an alliance between science and the arts has led many an artist astray—even the great Leonardo. Art is another kind of method, another way of looking at the world, than science. The artist is greatly concerned with his feelings, his visual and emotional judgments, and his personal mystique or vision.

We can observe this with Cézanne, who did a number of paintings of Mont Sainte-Victoire. For some reason, especially during the latter part of his life, this mountain utterly possessed

Cézanne's vision and imagination. Scientists could certainly have given him a great deal of information about it, but it is doubtful whether a thorough knowledge, even of geology, would have aided Cézanne in his painting. From the long series of paintings that Cézanne did of Mont Sainte-Victoire, it is evident that he hoped to find in his subject an affinity he had developed for the "mountain of his inner vision." His way was similar to that of a Zen master who attains his aim in the destruction of that aim.

Some artists, though, have made effective use of scientific methods to advance their art. The most common device among painters has been the use of what is known as the "golden section." Simply, this is a geometric way of dividing a line, or an area, into what is considered a pleasing harmonic proportion. Juan Gris and Jacques Villon are said to have made use of this, or of a similar method, and the De Stijl painter, Vantongerloo, has written of the mathematical ratios he employed in composing his paintings. In like manner, musicians have composed harmonic progressions, chords, and tonal values from mathematical ratios; Schillinger conceived a system for this purpose. In most cases a purely intellectual application of any arbitrary method will result in a sterile and lifeless work. It was really the visual judgment of Gris and Villon that enabled them to produce good work.

NEGATIVE SPACE AND VOLUME

Concerning the expanse of objects in space, painters have referred to that space in and around the objects as "negative space" and sometimes as "voids." In the counterpoise of negative space to the objects in a painting, the painter develops his personal volume. Volume may be defined as the simulated space each object occupies in a painting; it may also be considered as unique arrangements of space, but for purposes of clarity, we treat it as a separate entity.

As a primary consideration, the painter must consider the volume of objects jointly with the volume of the entire painting.

The old masters knew this well, which is a reason they achieved such a sense of fullness and unity in their paintings. In their large figural compositions, Rubens, Tintoretto, and Veronese often used what were called "end figures"—that is, objects painted very flat on the extreme sides of the painting (often appearing to be silhouettes), forming a contrast with the more voluminously modeled figures in the center area.

Sometimes the purpose of these painters is misunderstood. One of the authors remembers when, as a student in Paris, a friend of his returned from the Low Countries very disturbed because he had "discovered" Rubens was such a faulty draftsman. This painter failed to realize that although the figures in Rubens' paintings appear to be out of drawing, they are perfectly adjusted in the overall ensemble. Should some of the figures of El Greco, Rubens, and Tintoretto be brought to life we should really see an incredible tableau of misshapen individuals. But if such figures were not meant for this life, how well they live in the canvases of the masters!

In modeling volume the painter must observe an additional caution: he is not a sculptor who actually works in the round. In many of the academic works of the last century by such painters as Hippolyte Paul Delaroche, J. L. Gérôme, Sir Frederick Leighton, and John Singer Sargent, where modeling is dominant, the figures seem to be pieces of statuary glued onto the surface.

In some instances, even the greatest painters were not immune to this error. For example, in early works, when he was influenced by Caravaggio, Velásquez sometimes overrepresented his volumes. Notice how in his painting *The Water Carrier of Seville* a large earthen jug is modeled to resemble a bas-relief; this brings the space out of focus. In the later painting of Velásquez, such as *Supper at Emmaus*, we are not made aware of this spatial error.

In most modern approaches to painting, the painters do avoid heavy modeling in light and dark by the use of contrasting movements or overlapping planes around some focal point.

Velásquez, *The Water Carrier of Seville. Courtesy Wellington Museum, London*

Albrecht Dürer, *The Emperor Maximilian I.*

This is seen in the works of Picasso, Matisse, and Derain. (We
will discuss this problem again in our survey of Cubism.) Also,
when the volumes are overemphasized, it means the painter has
a number of gradations of grayed tones; this vitiates the force
of color. Volume in painting evokes the same sensation as in
music; it swells and recedes, but it is always there.

In this diagram from Dürer's woodcut *The Emperor Maximilian I*, space is treated as a void around and between solid
forms. The voids are also used for descriptive purposes, and
this spatial concept gives life and expression to the marvelous
portraits of the Romanesque, Gothic, and Renaissance styles.
Through the voids, as indicated by the arrows, the forms repre-
senting the positive or solid elements, in their exact relationship
to each other, establish the Emperor's features and dress. The
arrows indicating the negative space between the nose and the
cheekbone; the protuberance separating the nose and the hat;
the space between the man's underjaw and his chest; and the
space from the sloping shoulders to the background—all these
are fitted one to the other.

Rembrant and Seurat

In portraits, Rembrandt often makes a linear movement
through the subject's coat lapels to cut and modify the barrel-
like volume of the chest. There are figural portraits of Rembrandt that fill over three-fourths of the picture surface, yet
they never appear as pasted cutouts because subtle movements
up and across through the surface lock both the figures and
the backgrounds to the entire picture plane.

Seurat excelled in locking the volumes of his objects in
space. In this painting, *Young Woman Powdering Herself*, a
repetition of oval shapes is obvious, but less apparent is a complex of movements starting in the right arm of the woman
holding her powder puff and continuing through her right
breast. This same looping movement is repeated in the right
neckline of the dress and is carried across the woman's shoulders. The front edge of her dress repeats the movement in a

Rembrandt van Rijn, *Self-Portrait. Kunsthistorisches Museum, Vienna*

Seurat, Young Woman Powdering Herself. Courtauld Institute of Art, Home House Collection, London

vertical direction, and her left arm moves against these directions. It is the interaction of these varying movements that gives a sense of volume to the woman's torso and to the whole painting. As the eye of the observer encompasses the movements set against each other in opposing directions around a focal point he receives the illusion of fullness and volume.

MECHANICAL PERSPECTIVE: THE PICTORIAL ERROR

To project images into the arena of space, the most widely used convention in Western painting since the Renaissance has been mechanical perspective. Despite their limitation—the inability to project forms in space by the means of perspective alone—the space concepts formulated during the Renaissance are most understandable today: the camera lens is ground according to the principles of perspective, and the photographic image that is imposed on the minds of everyone has done much to curb our power to perceive volume and space.

The perception of space is a psychological as well as a visual phenomenon, and mechanical perspective, if applied in a strict logic, accounts for the world only in a flat, unimaginative way. For one reason, the observer is restricted to a fixed viewpoint that tends to create an exaggerated and disproportionate view of the true size of objects and their relationship to one another. Photographs taken with a hand or foot near the camera lens, whereby these appendages appear larger than the rest of the person's entire body, are an example of this shortcoming carried to a bizarre extreme. The Spanish poet Bécquer felt that photography lacked "that taste necessary to select what best suits the character of an object, that mysterious spirit, in short, that stands out in the work of a painter, which does not make an object just as it is, but as it appears to the imagination."

Today the photograph is acceptable as a credible facsimile of people and objects; this was not always so. In their *Journal of 1857* the Goncourts note an early auction of photographs in Paris with this comment, "Everything in this century is turning black, and is not photography the black vestment of the visible world?" Yet, to reexperience the world is difficult. The human mind has a way of adjusting to the thing at hand. Though we have learned to read black on white, this is the reverse of the way that black and white strike us in larger areas, where white advances and black recedes. When the average person attempts to read a blue-and-white photostat negative, he has great difficulty in doing so initially. People have learned to read a photograph, yet for most part something "more real" escapes them. It is like looking at pretty girls and not being able to see beautiful women.

The Pictorial Error

Mechanical perspective, with its device of projection by linear recession to one or more vanishing points, does open the picture surface, but if the scheme is carried out completely, it is almost impossible to close the surface again. Painters refer to these unrelieved thrusts into the surface as "holes." So when these gaping discrepancies on the picture plane are apparent, it is not possible to pacify all the spatial activity in order to achieve a unified picture. Delacroix said that genius must always change the tenets of perspective. Nevertheless, many of the great painters were criticized for doing so, especially during the eighteenth and nineteenth centuries, when the proponents of this method were everywhere.

Literally employed mechanical perspective produces the spatial effect of one or more tunnels that resemble megaphones seen from the large end, with the smaller end some distance from the front plane. With such a diminishing space it is difficult to control the full volumes of objects. The ground plane, on which the objects are placed, and the corresponding overhead plane, which compensates for their recession in distance, are manageable; but the volumes of objects on the far sides of the pictures are a cause for concern.

In this painting by Boutigny, the face and legs of Napoleon

F. Boutigny, *The Revolt at Pavia. Isaac Delgado Museum of Art, New Orleans*

are solid, but the torso beneath the folded arms is paper-thin. The open space at the top right portion of the picture, between the houses and the fortress, constitutes a gaping hole in the surface because it is unresolved by any countering movements.

In order to understand the problem of convergence on the picture plane, consider the following diagrams.

The first diagram shows the horizontal line with the lines of distance converging at a given point at the center. The second indicates a reversion into the picture plane that will converge at some point but not on the horizon line, thereby leaving the designer free to compose and close the plane. If the designer employs mechanical perspective, he will open the plane but will never be able to close it again because of the hole that punctures it.

SPATIAL CONVENTIONS

In turning now to a discussion of spatial conventions, we will follow, in respect to Western painting, chronological order, beginning with the late medieval era immediately preceding the Renaissance. Though it would be beyond the scope of this study to discuss every spatial manner, the Chinese concepts of space and art, which offer a profound contrast to Western ideals and a divergent unifying principle of structure and space, seem important enough to be included.

CUBIC SPACE

The term "cubic space" comes from the compositional method of using a rectangular cube, set obliquely on the picture plane, in terms of which the painting was developed. Although there are similarities of style in both manners, the method is not to be confused with twentieth-century Cubism for it was, in fact, a late-medieval method of construction used in the twelfth and thirteenth centuries, particularly in Italy, by such painters as Cimabue, Duccio, Lorenzetti, and Sassetta. Cubic space is a transition between flat Byzantine space and the receding space of the Renaissance.

Giovanni di Paolo, *St. Catherine of Siena and the Beggar. The Cleveland Museum of Art. Gift of the John Huntington Art and Polytechnic Trust*

After Giotto, painters became increasingly concerned with the problem of naturalism, and with the advent of the Renaissance, science and the rekindled humanism directed painting on yet another great adventure.

In *St. Catherine of Siena and the Beggar,* Di Paolo portrays a small room that dominates the painting as an oblique cube. The left side of the cube is a side wall, the right side is an open section from which the beggar enters. The narrow space ap-

Pietro Lorenzetti, *Life of the Blessed Humility. Uffizi, Florence*

Giovanni di Paolo, *Christ Carrying the Cross. The Walters Art Gallery,*
Baltimore

proximates that of the medieval stages, where miracle plays
and dumb shows were performed.

Practically all movements in space in this painting are
sharply diagonal planes to the right or to the left of the two
nuns. The space is imaginative and moving, despite the still-
ness of the figures and the firm architectural motifs.

An important compositional factor in this method is the
cadence of shifting and overlapping planes to suggest limited
depth. The interaction of the planes, moving in varying directions, gives volume to a flat surface. Imagine a sequence of

playing cards which you follow from right to left as one card overlaps another, and you will understand how the overlapping of planes can suggest movement and depth.

CHINESE AND ORIENTAL SPACE

The great Chinese painters developed a unique, rhythmic space directly related to calligraphy.* Rhythm and movement, essentials of calligraphy and painting alike, held meaning for the Chinese painter different from our understanding of these terms. To the Chinese, these attributes are essentials of a life force. By searching out rhythmical movements in rocks, mountains, and clouds, the painter followed what he believed to be the way of nature; he related its appearances more to his instincts than to his visual perception.

Such characteristics of Western painting as visual accuracy, chiaroscuro, and geometrical perspective held little appeal for the Chinese painter. Reality was not bound to a particular instance in time and space. The Chinese sought to know nature through universal and spiritual ways, and, in some instances, to experience its unity through sudden enlightenment.

In Chinese painting everything blends into a conceptual relationship. In this work by Wang Wei, we observe only a few rocks and the running surge of water breaking into waves at the foot of a waterfall. The rushing water is simply expressed, yet we feel its force and its mystery. Wang Wei realized perfectly the movement and rhythm of water and rocks as forms. Although only the essentials of the scene are presented, the viewer's imagination provides the connections between water, rock, and sky. Here, as in other great Chinese paintings, space is all-embracing; it is alive, dynamic, and the very soul of the painting.

In most oriental painting, and especially that of the Near East and India, distance is expressed by placing objects in

* Our concern is with the painters of the Classic periods: Tang Dynasty (A.D. 618–909), Five Dynasties (A.D. 907–960), Sung Dynasty (A.D. 960–1279), Yüan Dynasty (A.D. 1260–1368), and Ming Dynasty (A.D. 1368–1644).

Wang Wei, *Waterfall. Kyoto Museum*

the background higher on the picture plane. In this example
from a Persian painting, there is a suggestion of space, but in
effect there is background. The objects and forms rise in a
curve from the left of the picture upward, and descend in a
zigzag of verticals and horizontals from the upper left across
the building tops, and then precipitately downward, paralleling
the right side of the picture. The roosters atop the palace and
the calf's head in the second doorway from the left are no
larger in relation to the camels' or riders' heads at the bottom
and middle of the picture. The smaller planes overlap each
other in the same logical manner, rising from the left and
descending by way of the right. All these movements in space
are countered by curvilinear movements so that the two-
dimensional sovereignty of the plane is inviolate.

The space in Chinese painting seems to expand the farther
it is removed from man. Mountains, that in perspective would
recede, dominate the surface in some Sung paintings. The
painters did not look upon an object as only a form to be related to the scale of a painting; they shared an empathy with
all things in their vision. In old Chinese manuals on painting,
the author would often refer to the largest mountain in a range
as the father mountain with his children around him. Wang
Wei, one of the great poet-painters, expresses something very
similar in his *Notes on Painting*. "Paintings," he writes, "are not

Diagram from a Persian print.

produced by the mere exercise of manual skill; but upon completion must correspond to the phenomena of nature as explained in *The Book of Changes.*"*

There is a concept of space often referred to as "the law of
three sections." This scheme conceives the lower foreground
section of the painting as one would see it looking downward,
the middle section as if viewed from straight ahead, and the

---

* An ancient enigmatic Chinese book offering in diagram form what have
been interpreted as theories of the physical universe, and of moral and social
principles. Translated by Dr. Sukanishi.

In this print by the Japanese artist Sharaku, we see another facet of the proto-Cubist methods in Japanese art. In its rising and falling scheme of movements, there is a relationship to the Chinese philosophical concept of yin and yang.

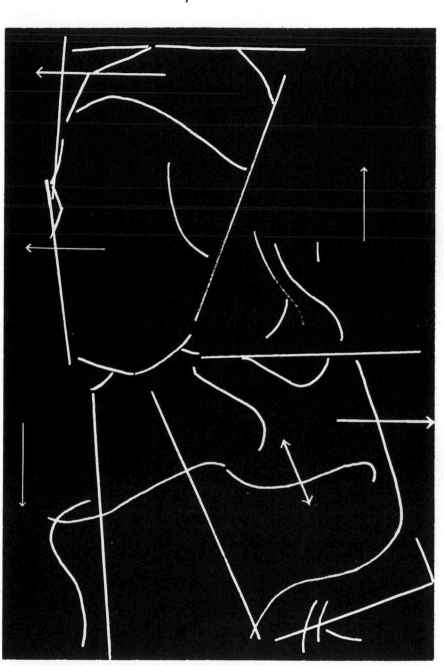

Chao-K'eh-hsiung, *Fish at Play*. Note the beautiful linear rhythms, the movements upward, downward, and to the sides in this Sung Dynasty painting. *The Metropolitan Museum of Art, New York. Kennedy Fund*

John Constable, *The White Horse. The Frick Collection, New York*

River Scene. In this lovely Ming Dynasty river scene, five distances are demarcated: the trees in the foreground, the boat, the marshes on the opposite shore, the distant hills, and the sun. The suggestion of distance is achieved by placing each higher on the picture. *The Metropolitan Museum of Art, New York. Fletcher Fund, 1947. The A. W. Bahr Collection*

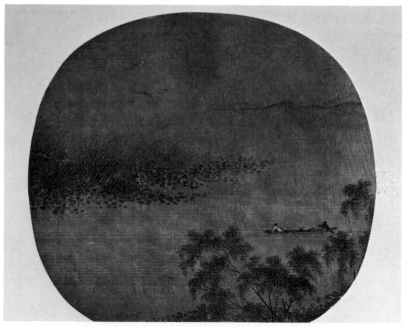

Li Ti, *Driving the Buffalo Homewards in the Snow. Courtesy Yamato Bunka-kan Collection, Japan*

Pieter Brueghel, *Winter. Kunsthistorisches Museum, Vienna*

upper part of the painting as if seen looking from the ground upward. The idea that these three spatial points are confined to Chinese painting is erroneous. This concept is more evident in Chinese painting because of the vertical format, and the simple descriptive character of most Chinese landscape painting. These three perspectives, combined in a single painting, exist in Western painting as well. However, the illusion of Western painting, with its aerial perspective, often prevents the observer from clearly distinguishing these simple relations.

In this Constable, the cow and the brook are viewed from above; the bridge is straight ahead at the viewer's eye level. The upper branches of the tree are seen as from below. The Chinese painter of *River Scene* does not make one conscious of such levels. Instead, he avoids complicating the visual effect.

The use of negative space, or voids, is uniquely handled in Chinese painting. The voids not only emphasize the scale of the painting (that is, the play of small areas against larger ones, the opposition of busy, or dense sections, against more placid areas) but also provide a resting place where the eyes and the mind can contemplate the painting. Chinese painting, based on a definite attitude toward man and nature, demands the full attention of the viewer for the very completion of the work.

To compare this attitude to a Western ideal, let us analyze these two snow landscapes: *Winter* by the Flemish painter Brueghel, and *Driving the Buffalo Homewards in the Snow* by Li Ti. Brueghel brings gifts of objective creation and conceptual thought to his landscape; Li Ti, the gifts of philosophic insight to his.

To detail accurately the effects of winter on man, and of man, at odds with his environment, Brueghel required a great sweep of pictorial space. One can go imaginatively through its expanse. Several men in the foreground, perhaps hunters or herdsmen, are returning home with their gaunt dogs. Beyond this group lies the activity of the village. People are warming themselves before a fire, while others are crossing a bridge.

Hans Holbein, *Sir
Thomas More. The
Frick Collection,
New York*

Albrecht Dürer, *The
Mourning for the
Dead Christ*—wood-
cut.

A marvelous bird, positioned perfectly in the painting, glides swiftly across the field. On a frozen pond in the distance, children and a few elders are skating. Far away, snow-covered crags ring the valley. We are convinced of the actuality of a sixteenth-century Flemish village on a winter day, where only the skating children seem to find any enjoyment.

The Li Ti painting does not offer the depth of space for the kind of journey undertaken with the Brueghel. Li Ti's painting is the world as seen in a golden mirror. One must look slowly about the painting, contemplating the space surrounding the trees and the foreground, just as Li Ti must have also reflected long on the essentials of this landscape. The ax-like strokes delineating the trees are set against a placid tan-gray background. Rhythmic incisive strokes that texture the bullock are contrasted with light touches in the foreground. The branches directly above the man appear calligraphic, as if Li Ti had organized the strokes into a poem about the winter. There is an old Chinese saying that "the artist must hold the Universe in his hand." In this work the bull and the man do seem eternal.

RENAISSANCE SPACE

To Renaissance thinkers like Alberti, Copernicus, and Tartaglia, phenomena could be explained by physical, mechanical, and mathematical laws. The belief that these laws were directly related to man's purpose on earth and to his welfare stimulated the minds of artists, scientists, and philosophers until well into the nineteenth century, when the primacy of science was fully asserted in Western culture.

The idea that the world could be subjected to the discipline of the mind was one reason why painters employed geometrical perspective in logically accounting for all they saw before them. Painting was another window opening onto the world. Renaissance painters shared with their Chinese confreres the profound observation of nature, although, as we have indicated, for different reasons. The Renaissance artist often became enthusiastic over studies of plant life and mechanics, apart from any usefulness these studies might contribute to his art. Most of us are familiar with Leonardo's interest in physics and the other sciences. Titian, or one of his assistants, illustrated Vesalius' famous book on anatomy. Only at the end of a letter he wrote in seeking employment does Leonardo mention his ability to paint a likeness. The Renaissance artist, along with his fellows, wanted to see life from varying viewpoints and to transcend the heretofore ecclesiastic, finite way of thinking and existing whereby men were enjoined to see in nature a sign of God's omnipresence and the truth of religion.

As the organ of visual perception, the eye is symbolic of Renaissance concern with problems of optics and space. Receding perspective was rapidly developed by Alberti, Dürer, Della Francesca, Leonardo, Pacioli, Uccello, and a number of other architects, geometricians, and painters. By the sixteenth century, exact rules for projection, vanishing points, and foreshortening had been formulated. By that time, painters had the means to solve such major problems of perspective as the rendering of figures and architectural vistas from any angle. Following the decline of the Italian Renaissance, and on through the eighteenth century, most Europeans saw perspective as contingent with space. This confusion of space with perspective made for great problems, so that good painters, like Dürer and Tintoretto, had to alter the laws of perspective whenever these canons interfered with their design. In its original sense, perspective was not involved with spatial volume; it only placed objects in distance.

The revived concepts of Euclidean geometry utilized in formulating the canons of perspective were also a keystone of the intellectual tradition, from Copernicus to Descartes, that changed our world. In their desire to know the world, many scientists of the time reasoned that the world was essentially mathematical in structure; Kepler even felt that God had created the world in terms of perfect numbers. What the thoughtful man saw, he wanted answers for. It had been a

This engraving after Raphael's *Paul and Barnabas at Lystra* accentuates the great elements of Renaissance space and structure.

long medieval night, and people were interested in unraveling whatever mystery they could. The Renaissance artists, in their approach, were animated by the same desire and their work, particularly that of the Dutch School, gives information about people, and the possessions of these people, about historical events, and about the events of Holy Scripture.

Patrons of art during the Renaissance were also concerned with the representation of receding space. They would often counsel their friends as to the place to stand before a painting in order to secure the most lifelike effect. Sometimes the place was marked on the floor. Filippo Brunelleschi, the architect,

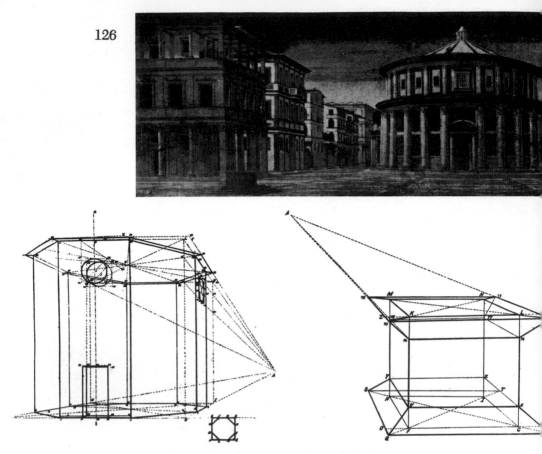

Perspective drawings by Piero della Francesca

did a painting of a city square in perspective, similar to this painting by another architect, Luciano da Laurana. At the point of the observer's eyeline Brunelleschi drilled a hole through the picture; when one looked through the peephole from the rear side into a mirror held in front of the painting the sensation was comparable to looking at the actual scene.

In Renaissance painting we observe another difference: figures were set in space in an essentially democratic way. No longer did the painter portray the king, or the saint, two or three times larger than other less exalted personages. The important figure was centered, but one could see that he was subject to the same physical law as others. In this, Renaissance painters were also influenced by the impact of humanism.

Architectural perspective drawing by Luciano da Laurana

Note the projection of object, the close-up view, in Bronzino's *Lodovico Capponi. The Frick Collection, New York*

Michelangelo, *The Brazen Serpent. Vatican, Vatican City*

Leonardo wrote that he doubted the advisability of rendering in detail all objects in a painting, since he observed that figures and objects in the middle and far distance appear to dissolve in the atmosphere.

Despite their use of perspective, the essential attribute of Renaissance paintings was that of "nearness." This is not a paradox, but an aim of these painters, influenced by humanism, of presenting a close-up view of the main elements in a painting: the person portrayed, his clothing, his jewelry, and other ornaments. The person and his world were brought forward to enlighten the observer as to his phenomenal existence. The *Mona Lisa,* the *Alba Madonna,* and *St. George Fighting the Dragon* were presented full stage. The landscape and the architectural features of the painting formed a properly ordered background in space.

The Renaissance painters were the great craftsmen of painting, and they favored the perfection of details. Though they did not use the brisk, vigorous brushwork of a Rembrandt or Goya, the high finish of Renaissance painting, in the work of its greatest masters, is not the result of pedantry. It is the result of an insistence on perfection in presenting the world of objects as seen by a superior mind and specially trained observer.

BAROQUE SPACE

Michelangelo, often seen as one of the culminating glories of the Renaissance, is in effect the master who heralded its turning point. In the passionate and often unfinished volumes of his last sculptures, in the restless and flamelike action of his frescoes (especially such works as *The Brazen Serpent* and *The Punishment of Haman*) were born the mannerisms of the baroque style.* Heinrich Wölfflin, the nineteenth-century historian, regarded the baroque as a dissolution of Renaissance style; we see today that it was something else. It did no less than establish a new vision and a new space.

Michelangelo was critical of the minute detail and enamel-like finish of early Renaissance painting, especially that of Flemish painting. He has been quoted as saying of Flemish painting, "In short this art is without power and without distinction; it aims at rendering minutely many things at the same time, of which a single one would have sufficed to call forth a man's whole application." But as Huizinga explains in *The Waning of the Middle Ages*, "It was the Medieval spirit itself which Michelangelo judged here."

The great baroque painters lived in the time of Balboa, Champlain, De Soto, and other great voyagers and explorers—restless men who sailed their ships far past the fixed horizons

* The height of baroque influence lasted roughly from 1600 to 1750, varying in different countries.

Giovanni Battista Tiepolo, *The Crucifixion. City Art Museum of Saint Louis*

of their precursors. In like manner, the baroque artists explored their kind of expanding world.

The violence and expanse of this age of discovery found expression not only in painting and exploration, but in all of life. The overall space concept of this era was not one of nearness but, rather, one of great distance. Many have felt the baroque period was revolting because of the pomp and ceremony associated with it. During a discussion in which one of the authors participated, a panel member observed that this period was a time when social and cultural affairs were manipulated like toys by two or three hundred nobles. A rejoinder was made that, on the contrary, this was not unlike the state-subsidized art of today. It is true that, in the baroque period, almost everyone went to the churches, heard the baroque music, and participated in the unbelievably grandiose funerals and public festivals.

By the seventeenth century, the Renaissance flame was dimming. The spirit of intellectual and physical activity that had begun in the Renaissance further loosened the restrictive tenets of the Church and of an authoritarian society. Riches found in the New World flowed to the old continent, creating a promise of real luxury and the effervescent desire for grandeur. The relatively modest homes of the Renaissance gave way to huge edifices. Even in the more simply designed, less embellished baroque churches, especially those in Bavaria and Austria, the sunlight and blue sky entered into the architectural whole through large pane-glass windows. Heavy confining stained-glass windows, used in the Gothic era, were seldom found in baroque churches. Altar paintings were arranged to suggest an enormous cluster of flowers encircling the altar. In the spatial drama of baroque painting the tendency was to paint the main figural groups in the middle distance; figures and architectural objects in the extreme foreground resemble silhouettes against a lighted stage where the drama begins beyond the proscenium arch.

A typical baroque interior

Enormous rooms, such as the baroque interior shown here, were decorated in a seemingly endless profusion of designs. Walls were ornamented so as to dissolve the very physical confines of the rooms. A profusion of mirrors and highly polished floors caused the hundreds of lighted candles, held in prismal chandeliers, to be multiplied endlessly. Marbled staircases were designed in winding arabesques, so that the up and downward movement of the stairs would appear continuous. Paintings done on the walls were ingeniously joined with the architecture. Often the drapery of a painted figure was molded of wood and plaster, and sometimes the head of a figure would be executed as a bas-relief, so that the head could pass beyond the end of a wall. In this way the particular space of the wall was sacrificed in order to unify the complete space of the room.

In the Venetian opulence of the baroque, the desire for well-being was expressed everywhere. Madonnas and saints beckoned the faithful from roseate skies, and the sinister characters of the entombment and purgatory were referred to only when it was unavoidable. People traveled and moved not in hopes of finding St. Augustine's "City of God," but bold and confident of finding El Dorado.

This confidence and bravado are illustrated in a story told of Tintoretto. At a gathering of artists in Venice where he was present, one group generously praised a portrait by Titian. When he returned home, Tintoretto took an oil sketch, covered it with lampblack, and painted a head in Titian's manner. At the next gathering, he showed the small painting as an original Titian. Everyone believed it so, until Tintoretto revealed what he had done. The audacity and ability of many great spirits of the time are amply typified in Tintoretto.

One of the most energetic and productive major talents in the history of Western art, Tintoretto was able to conjure from the styles of Titian and Michelangelo his own poetic and tempestuous style, comparable in scope to the mature Shakespeare of *The Tempest* and *The Winter's Tale.*

Tintoretto, *The Massacre of the Innocents. Scuola di San Rocco, Venice*

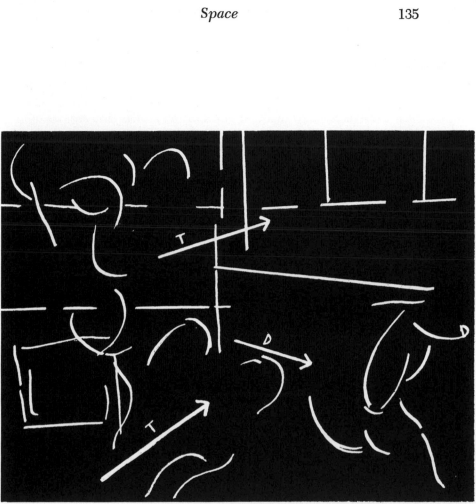

Baroque rhythms.

In construction, Tintoretto's large figural compositions appear as if seen from the first balcony of a theatre. And extending the analogy between Tintoretto's painting and the drama, it is known that he made small settings, with tiny figures and architectural elements, as a guide in planning his compositions.

Like a stage designer, Tintoretto lighted these sets from various points to determine the fall of light and shadow. (For now the shadows were on man's face, and something of his inner world was reflected in the visual world of light. This "divine shadow," however, meant that man would increasingly be concerned with transient values and would certainly reconcile his place in time and space with what values he assigned to history.)

Consider one of Tintoretto's best-known paintings, *The Massacre of the Innocents*. The canvas is huge and the subject has been dramatically, even violently, conceived. One observes the common attributes of the baroque style: the funneling space, the pyramid construction of the figural groups, and the serpentine linear movement through individual figures. Few observers of the baroque period, however, seem to recognize the discipline of its masters—especially in their geometric organization, in the shift of great planes, and in the tight underlying structure that served to control their vertiginous designs, allowing the separate units of the paintings to compose into an organic whole.

The diagram based on *The Massacre of the Innocents* indicates the large simple planes underlying the swirling baroque rhythms. Note how Planes T move into depth, while Planes D demonstrate a subtle shift in the planar movement that contains the composition in the frontal area. Baroque concepts were only slightly modified, but definitely impoverished, at the time of the French Revolution. The baroque period ended during the reign of Louis XV with the "Louisiana Bubble," when the whole financial structure of France toppled.

The rococo style, which developed later, followed the passionate drama of the Revolution; then this style, too, was subjected to drastic change for by then the admirers of Watteau had long embarked for the island of Cythera, and Fragonard was living in poverty. David and his neo-Classicist followers sought their inspiration in the classic ideal of Greek sculpture and the work of Raphael. Afterward, the Romanticists, led by Delacroix, sought to enliven the color and drama of painting —creative baroque elements threatened by the puritanism of neo-Classicism—and subsequently the Naturalists, of whom the most outstanding was Courbet, altered subject matter in its entirety by utilizing themes previously thought unfit for painting. Finally, the Impressionists and post-Impressionist painters, in their efforts to render nuances of color corresponding to those of nature, found new ways of accounting for volume and space.

THE ACADEMIC ERROR OF THE NINETEENTH CENTURY

The nineteenth-century academicians were not all born simultaneously but they all ended in the boneyard of art, despite David and Ingres' guideposts of good intentions. During and immediately following the period of Impressionism, the resemblance in painting to the mechanical vision of photography was at its worst. This can be seen in the monster, and often monstrous, compositions of such academic professors as Delaroche, Baudry, and Tissot. Despite what Baudelaire wrote of such painters, that they carried out no tradition except their own, many of their troubles can be traced to a misconception of Renaissance style or baroque style—in particular the fantastic perspective inventions of Tiepolo.

These inventions, especially those that showed the so-called "worm- or frog-eyed view," can be seen in many ceiling paintings, systematized and completely devoid of the artistry of great decorators like Veronese and Tiepolo. Baudry's garish designs for the ceiling and proscenium arch of the Paris Opera

House come to mind. Whether or not the temporary ceiling decorations of Chagall, which were placed over Baudry's originals, are any improvement is a matter of conjecture—even though they were commissioned by André Malraux, in a French version of the contemporary cultural explosion.

The academicians often lifted whole groupings and separate figures from Raphael and Giulio Romano. Peter von Cornelius, the German nineteenth-century painter, painted a mural commission in Munich at the Glyptothek. Not having exactly the same space areas to work with as did Raphael, Cornelius had to invent certain figures. But in his inventions he gives himself away. Cornelius could copy what he saw; however, he could not work in the same spirit as the Renaissance painters. Neither could his contemporaries, Benjamin Constant, Sir Frederick Leighton, James Tissot, and a host of others whose works filled the salons of the nineteenth century. With such painters, the greatest brutalities in the whole history of art were inflicted upon the picture plane. The camera has never so crassly exaggerated the scale of a picture as did these "masters of the salon." Here painting ceased to be painting and became the forerunner of the Hollywood spectacles of Cecil B. De Mille.

In an attempt to equivocate errors, or a lack of spatial organization, it became necessary for the academicians to avoid the very problems that Rubens and Velásquez had faced and solved. Whenever possible, painters emptied the foregrounds and grouped the highly lighted figures in the middle distance, somewhat in the manner of the baroque painters but without their genius for spatial organization. The color of most salon pieces was reduced to a monotone, and a rigid semblance of composition was established.

If these painters tried to solve their immediate spatial problems through hedging and discretion in the large salon pieces, it was in the smaller paintings that their basic faults were never modified. The lack of sensory response to pictorial organization

Gustave Boulanger, *The Woman's Court. Isaac Delgado Museum of Art, New Orleans*

Nicholas Poussin, *The Baptism of Christ. John G. Johnson Collection,*
Philadelphia

Jacques Louis David, *Comtesse Daru. The Frick Collection, New York* ➤

is apparent in portraits where three pink spots, the face and the two hands of the sitter, appear in hundreds of academic portraits as three unconnected outposts in a vast desert of gray and brown paint.

Unable to compose the connecting shapes and movement, these painters buried embarrassing areas in layers of bitumin and lava. Aside from such technical mishaps, the illustrative and sentimental approach of the academicians to their subject matter weakened any serious consideration of their painting.

David and Ingres revived some of the classical methods of Poussin and Raphael, and even painted some of the same subjects as did these Renaissance masters; but later in the century an unfortunate misconception of the classic ideal produced such travesties as *The Woman's Court* by Gustave Boulanger.

IMPRESSIONIST SPACE

The Impressionist problem was no longer one of Classicism versus Romanticism (in essence, the precisely defined shape as opposed to the painterly flow of color) that had led to the dispute between Ingres and Delacroix. It was an intense searching for knowledge to support new discoveries in color and aesthetics. Manet studied Hals and the Spanish painters. Degas, Monet, and other Impressionists applied the pattern and flat asymmetrical space of Japanese wood-block artists such as Hiroshige, Hokusai, and Utamaro.*

Initially, the Impressionists were as much in revolt against academic painting as they were in pursuit of their own values. In mid-nineteenth-century France, state patronage went to painters like Gérôme and Meissonier. Because of this, and for social and political reasons, many of the Impressionists held in

---

* We have now learned that these seemingly casual color prints are deceptive in a spatial sense, for Hiroshige and Hokusai were the last masters of a long and definitive tradition.

contempt the state and the official institutions of art. When, later in the century, public recognition did come, most of the Impressionists declined an offer of honorary decoration.

The Impressionists did not want to paint gods or saints: their subjects were people at a picnic, people walking along the avenues, people at the racetrack, and people boating—these everyday activities and pleasures together with simple landscapes. When they did paint an imaginary picture, as Manet did of a woman dressed as a toreador, the picture had a certain wit: no one was supposed to believe the lady was a bullfighter. Later, after a visit to Spain, Manet became fascinated and intrigued by the color and activity of the bullring, however, and did a number of drawings and paintings of actual scenes of *corridas*.

After Constable, nature became everyone's concern: depicting nature replaced emulating Raphael. Each painter met the challenge in a different way. The Impressionist, tired of the classical lady in her nightgown with her bow and arrows, decided to paint an actual woman as the huntress. In this case, the painter changed his approach to painting more than his approach to nature.

The Impressionist technique seemed to call for a naturalistic subject. A German Impressionist, Albert Weisgerber, did a rather remarkable and symbolic painting of St. Sebastian in the woods. The painting has a contradiction: the observer is made to feel that the saint is without an inner light and that, in the material light of Impressionism, he is dissolving along with the faith that initially inspired this traditional religious subject.

When, early in his career, Manet painted the Christ figure supported by two angels, it was more of a solid work inspired by Goya, Murillo, and Velásquez. Manet was possibly the last great painter to paint successfully in the grand manner, although his work was on the highest level of virtuosity. Courbet, his immediate predecessor, once criticized Manet's flatly painted surfaces as, "always with the same playing cards." Manet's reply was, "and with you, my friend, always the same three billiard balls."

The casual admirer of Manet is probably unaware of the architectural two-dimensional structure underlying his painting. His paintings have the appearance of a complete and irresponsible spontaneity, which was what Manet intended. However, the student of painting will do well to observe how the salient points of the shapes are subject to horizontal and vertical lines that divide the canvas into a structure of strong and pleasing proportion.

HORIZONTAL AND VERTICAL CONTROL

The apparent casualness of Manet's work hid a great compositional complexity. In the following three variations on a similar theme, he demonstrates his exceptional horizontal and vertical control—one of the profound aspects of structure.

In *The Café Singer*, the steplike character of the planes indicated should not be conceived of as an arrangement of planes in recession from front to back, but as a network that, in emphasizing the rectangular character of the surface, welds it into one plane. Technically, this unification of the plane surface is known as closure; its appearance when analyzed resembles a grid. This method helps to unify an agitated surface by establishing "rests," comparable to pauses in music or to the division of notes in a bar of music.

In *At the Café*, the incomplete nature of the drawing delineating the gentleman's left arm, crooked over the cane in his right hand, is but another aspect of Manet's vision. What appear to be errors in drawing in a number of his works, in fact, are fully explained in the way he relates individual parts to the overall concept. Manet reveals objects as they appear to the naked eye—and to the eye alone—and he was completely aware that

this way of seeing could be a vital part of his impression. Therefore, if the arms of the man in this painting seem crowded in
the space, this was done intentionally. Such positional devices
appear ever more frequently in Manet's later work. Note how
in this case he employs a twisting of figural objects for the
purpose of locking an asymmetrical space.

Now note in this version, *Au Café,* how the massing of forms
does not require the same extended closure to unify the painting as was observed in the other two works by Manet. It is
rather obvious, though, that the line of the girl's hair if completely continued would join with an object, seemingly a match
holder, on the table. This directional can be interpreted as a
kind of closure.

Here the objects are united by a group of generally vertical
rectangles moving against the background—a horizontal rectangle. In addition, the unrepeated diagonal of the table,
through the rather mysterious opposing diagonals of the central figures of the man and woman, hold perfectly in the space.
It might be observed that the cane held by the gentleman is
not the axis of this diagonal movement; it is the plane, bounded
by the shadow on the woman's coat and the left contour of the
man's coat, which gives the exact opposition to the table. Actually, the cane picks up the top of the other man's hat to form
an enormous triangle.

Along with Manet, the other Impressionists realized that the
action of pure color was most effective in a shallow space. This
is true in Egyptian wall painting, in Persian miniatures, and
with most expressions where color is of prime importance. With
experience, the Impressionists discovered the spatial limitations
of linear perspective, though they did not break with the
system. In the later nineteenth century these painters moved

Édouard Manet, *The Café Singer. National Gallery, London*

Édouard Manet, *At the Café. Courtesy of Walters Art Gallery, Baltimore*

Édouard Manet, *Au Café. Collection Oskar Reinhart am Römerholz,*
Winterthur, Switzerland

toward a space where color, as perspective, was the most significant factor. When we consider the direction that painting has taken today, the most fortuitous factor in Impressionist color theory was that these methods were steps leading to the modern abstraction of color.

The Impressionists were poets of light and color, and the color nuance as related to the colors of nature was an essential of their space. Many Impressionist works reflected observations of nature under certain circumstances of light, such as Monet's translations of Chartres Cathedral and of haystacks, done at different hours of the day. The Impressionists, however, were not literal translators of nature.

When first shown as a group in Paris during 1874, 1876, and 1877, their works caused riots of disapproval. In fact, the designation "Impressionist" was adopted then as a term of derision. Our acceptance of this way of painting came only when we accepted the Impressionist convention of color and space—the same way the Florentines, accustomed to flat Byzantine space, finally accepted Giotto.

If Impressionism was a negation of the classical attitude, it was in no sense a negation of the physical life surrounding its painters. People now refer to the pleasure-giving appearance of Impressionist painting—though in its own day, apparently, such work was not considered pleasurable; in fact, the subject matter of the Impressionist paintings was often considered rather vulgar.

POST-IMPRESSIONIST SPACE

With Cézanne there is the culmination of the kind of painting that Manet managed so well. This extremely sensitive painter no longer chose to see with the fragmentary and surface vision of most Impressionists. To him, all things in nature were growing and developing in relation to each other. Accordingly, Cézanne rejected full perspective in favor of precise color modulation and the balance and tension of planes.

To realize his sensations, Cézanne had to become a truly unique painter. In fact, he comes close to those Chinese painters who contemplated nature a long time before executing the landscape from an inner vision. Cézanne applies various classical compositional methods to the study of color, subject matter, and space, resolving his shapes in an austere, geometric way and, as we observed in the chapter on structure, using a linking arabesque linear movement to connect these shapes. He avoided effects such as rays of sunlight, moonlight, mist, and diffused lighting. Although he retained a motif from nature, Cézanne learned to create without any rigid, preconceived, romantic concept of the motif, as he did—often with disturbing effect—in his early works.

Cézanne's aversion to having people touch him was almost paranoia, as was his suspicious reaction to favorable comments about his work; but fortunately he was equally hypersensitive to all visual and tactile impressions. Although he referred to his painting, in false modesty, as my "little sensation," it was this sensibility that enabled him to realize his unique and monumental qualities as a painter. In an illuminating article, Maurice Merleau-Ponty quotes this revealing comment by Cézanne: "Balzac describes in his 'Wild Ass's Skin' a tablecloth as white as a blanket of new-fallen snow on which the glasses rose vertically, the knives and forks lay horizontally and the whole was crowned by yellow rolls. Throughout my youth, I wanted to paint that tablecloth of new-fallen snow. I know now that one must will to paint only: the table things arose symmetrically and yellow rolls. If I paint 'crowned' I am up a tree, understand? And if I balance and shade my cloths and rolls truly as in nature, be sure the crowning, the savor, and all the trembling will be there."

The man who said this knew the important thing in painting was to find the way. For Cézanne, this meant the proper manipulation of color and form corresponding to his concept of the forces of nature. When Cézanne painted a white house

Claude Monet, *Cap Martin near Menton. Courtesy Museum of Fine Arts, Boston. Julia Cheney Edwards Collection*

Paul Cézanne, *Still Life*. Note how in this canvas Cézanne demonstrates his sure knowledge of baroque structure, in the use of both the arabesque and the planar support to give stability and punctuation to the design. In principle, as well as phenomenally, Cézanne's painting resembles Tintoretto's *The Massacre of the Innocents*, shown earlier. *National Gallery of Art, Washington, D.C. Chester Dale Collection, 1962*

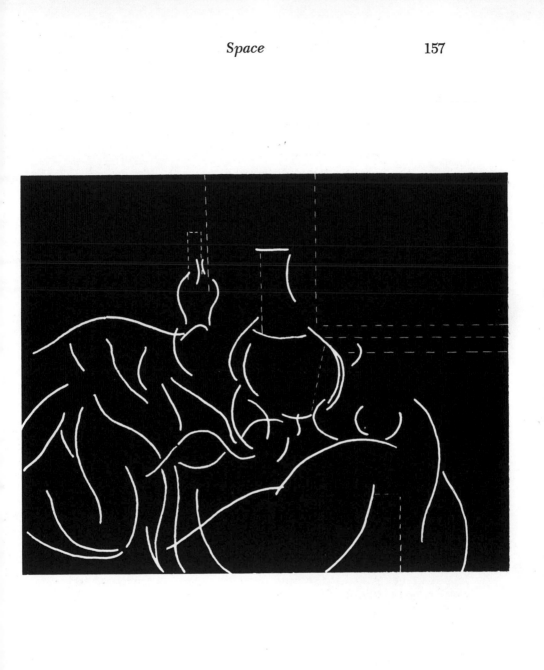

Paul Cézanne, *Mont Sainte-Victoire*. A landscape poorly designed and composed can make a mountain in the distance appear as an insignificant hillock. In the Cézanne shown here, all the landscape is a subdivision and support for the big silhouette covering seven-eighths of the canvas. The monumentality of the mountain is enhanced but not disturbed. *Philadelphia Museum of Art. George W. Elkins Collection*

against a blue sky, the white and the blue were considered as colors relating not only to each other, but to the field of color surrounding them. When the color planes were poised and fully related within the space, the white became a house, the blue, a sky.

Cézanne's paintings are monumental even when compared to other great works of his time. This holds true whether the painting is a mountain or a bowl of apples, because Cézanne relates all parts of the painting into one surface, something only a few had been able to accomplish since the time of the baroque painters. With maturity, he overcame all previous considerations of objects in space by concentrating on the relationship of color and movement. His color is so carefully adjusted in movement and in contrast that his space and form become one—consistent and inseparable. This mobile form of composition is his great contribution to modern painting.

Cézanne's unfinished or abandoned canvases of the Mont Sainte-Victoire period show the growth of space from free movements in horizontal, vertical, and diagonal brushstrokes that begin at one or a number of points on the surface. These unfinished paintings may have been so terrifying in their implications that the aging master might simply have decided he did not wish to complete them at the time. It is conceivable that the genius of Cézanne outdistanced his faith in the miracles he was beginning to achieve.

After Cézanne, a painting became an experience to be enjoyed on its own terms. The work of art was no longer the performance of a virtuoso, and the space was an end result; it was not the point of departure as in previous centuries.

Seurat's approach to painting was different from Cézanne's —quite different. The scientific method was second nature to Seurat, since he felt an orderly method freed his creative powers rather than limited them. Matisse said that Seurat was the first artist to make an order of Impressionist discoveries. Though Seurat was a systematic and logical painter, he was actually less logical than Cézanne in procedure. Seurat left works of great beauty, but an unwitting compromise is evident in the discrepancy between his flat ornamental drawing and his finished painting, in which he positioned objects in perspective into a preconceived, shallow, saucer-like space.

Given a longer life, Seurat (who died at thirty-two) would certainly have forsaken this illustrative quality, because it was so markedly at variance with his compositional principles. Seurat once said that the art of painting was "the art of hollowing out a canvas." There is much to be said for this dictum, but Seurat hollowed out too deep a space—which fortunately, was not so in his drawings. Painting is an art of putting something over something else, the silhouette moving over and against another form. Cézanne understood this, and he did not value Seurat highly—but then Cézanne did not value any of his contemporaries highly: he was much too preoccupied with his own demons. Yet Seurat is a descendant of everything elegant in French art, and without him it is doubtful that the direction of formal painting would have continued as it did with Cubism.

The Bathers, one of Seurat's earliest large-scale compositions, shows his concern with the stylization and casualness of Impressionist painting. The backs of the two seated boys, together with the one calling in the water, are developed in a rather obvious repetition of curved accents. The difference in the archaic style of this simplification with that of the reclining figure and the clothes of the bather, and the manner in which the other figures and objects were developed, seems mildly contradictory. Ultimately, the work, with all its quality and refinement, represents a young artist who had not yet entirely resolved the differences between the conceptual and the perceived.

CUBIST SPACE

Cubism is a resolution of forms, largely taken from the works of Cézanne and Seurat, with self-imposed limitations as to

Seurat, *The Bathers. The National Gallery, London*

164

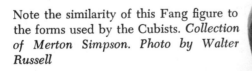

Note the similarity of this Fang figure to the forms used by the Cubists. *Collection of Merton Simpson. Photo by Walter Russell*

subject matter, color, and the amount of volume revealed. The Cubists were also influenced by non-European forms, an interest which began with the romantic movement of the nineteenth century.

Once the prejudice against the cultivated art of the Orient was overcome, there was recognition for the art of all peoples, even for the art of those living in so-called primitive surroundings. Since all artists in their own way explore the wisdom of the ages, the Cubists found in African sculpture, with its non-Hellenistic proportions, an art that gave their movement a spiritual impetus. Although this influence is disputed by many today (including some of the Cubists of the first heroic period), it remains true. The primitive influence was aesthetic and expressive rather than technical; this may be why it is now being discredited.

With Cubism came another turning point: the end of nature worship. Painters thereafter consulted nature for knowledge, but did not bow or defer to it. Cubism has its roots in the scientific and rationalistic culture of the twentieth century; its disciples understood nature in a more materialistic way than did artists of the previous century.

After Cézanne and Seurat, it was inevitable that the Cubist would arrive at a shallow space. In Cubist painting, space became as real an element as the jars, tables, and guitars that comprised its subject matter. In continuing the development of their space, Cubists such as Picasso and Gris ultimately placed thin planes one above the other, arranging them in a progression from the central plane back toward the four corners. Curves were opposed by countercurves, or movements set in opposing directions; sometimes half-curves were set against flat areas. These flat areas were modulated by shading, to give the areas density and to separate individual areas from each other.

The depth of Cubist space is relatively simple. Assuming Renaissance space to be concave, Cubist space is convex, very

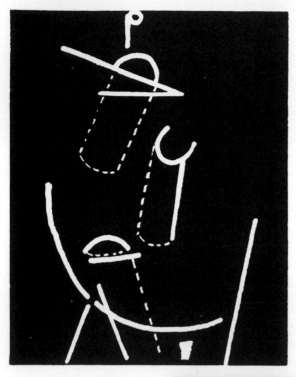

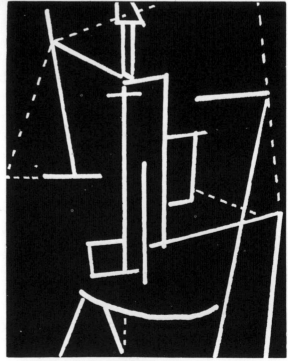

In early Cubism, frequently called the Heroic
Period and lasting from about 1906 to 1912, the
volume and plane were implied by suggestion.
Note the application of this in these three diagrams from Picasso still lifes. In the first, the
dotted lines complete the cylinder. In the next
two, the dotted lines indicate the planes. In the
last, the repetition of triangles in various sizes is
emphasized, and the dotted lines complete some
of the triangles. Needless to say, the division of
the whole plane and the accents affecting that
plane are also demonstrated.

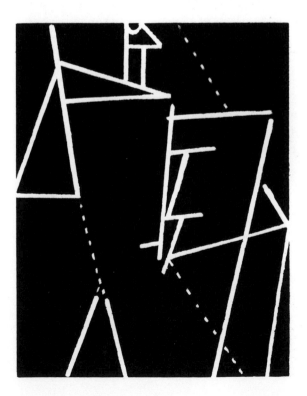

much like an umbrella turned inside out. With the deepest plane in the depth of the painting pulled forward, imagine looking into a room where the floor could pivot upward to an 80- or 85-degree arc from the original position. Picasso's *The Three Musicians* offers a fine illustration of the shallow space involved in Cubist painting—a space similar to the "cubic" space of medieval times.

Once the painter became less concerned with representation, the repetition of small hooks, curves, and superimposed planes was employed to unify and animate the tactile and plastic character of the surface. Because of the Cubist use of semi-diagonal planes and movements, and countermovements of overlapping planes, unresolved fragments of such planes were often left at the extremities of the picture surface. This was a shortcoming that Juan Gris rarely overcame.

Geometric shapes—mainly triangles, rectangles, and rhomboids—were repeated with diverse accent. A triangle, for instance, might be used as a white accent and then again as a black or a gray one. The tonally overshaded edges in some Cubist works sometimes suggest a Caravaggio-like, chiaroscuro effect; this phenomenon is also evidenced in the work of the Futurists and refutes their claim to a "total revolt from the past." Picasso and other Cubists countered this effect by leaving the corners light and darkening the center mass. Interestingly, a series of Picasso's best early Cubist paintings appears to portray Gothic cathedrals in a gray mist.

DECORATIVE CUBISM

The second, or decorative, stage of Cubism was developed out of a rhomboid shape. The heretofore small central plane was increased to cover a considerable area of the painting. This plane was placed in a semidiagonal position, supported by other movements to establish a diamond shape. The points of this shape touched the four sides of the painting at the center of

Juan Gris, *Dish of Fruit. Philadelphia Museum of Art. A. E. Gallatin Collection*

Pablo Picasso, *Ma Jolie (Woman with a Zither or Guitar).*
Collection, The Museum of Modern Art, New York. Lillie
P. Bliss Bequest

We chose to diagram this still life by Picasso ➤
because of the unequivocal clarity of his use
of the diamond control. In this canvas, the
sides of the diamond are fashioned inside the
borders of the four sides; this was done, apparently, to provide an unagitated border and
to circumvent the necessity for any fragmented
pieces along the edges of the painting.

each side. The diamond shape as a control is constantly evidenced in Cubism, but it is usually obscured by a number of other movements. In this particular painting, Picasso has given a synthesis of three characteristic elements of Cubism in their simplest forms.

(1) He has used the step-angle in the four corners and again in the central plane;

172

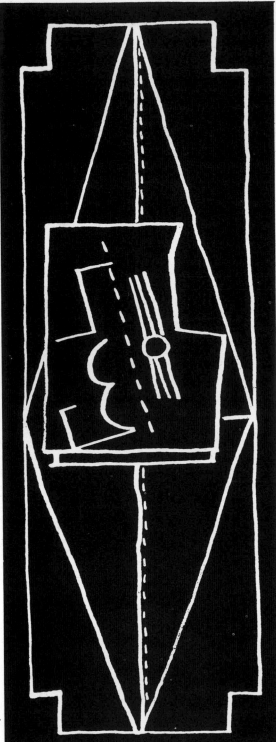

This diagram illustrates another and very obvious instance of Picasso's diamond control.

(2) the diamond shape is here used quite obviously;

(3) the axis of the inside center plane is turned. This is suggested by the three guitar strings, a zigzag, and a hook moving away from the axis of the vertical axis of the picture itself.

Simple objects and interiors were most frequently used as motifs. These objects could be satisfactorily described by a simple outline, and this generally ruled out such a complex volume as the human figure. The images were presented clearly in the space, since the representative aim was to describe and to avoid any illusion. Multiple space aspects of objects were presented and not, as was often erroneously stated, multiple views of the same subject; the early work of Marc Chagall, who *did* dismember his subjects, is a conspicuous exception.

Picasso's two versions of *The Three Musicians* are the culmination of decorative, or ornamental, Cubism. They are based on the static, formal arrangements found in Inca or Mayan textiles. Thereafter, Picasso and Braque, the masters of the style, developed their own individual approaches.

This Braque is one of the choice examples of decorative Cubism. There is no need for an extended comment on the action of the superimposed planes—the form repetition in the various objects and the contrast of the central mass with the table. Therefore, we shall simply observe that the black plane above the checkered plane seems calculated to give depth to the still life. The three planes at the bottom of the painting— the dark plane in front of the checkered one, the checkered plane, and the black plane immediately above it—are rhythmically arranged from the base of the painting upward in a circular movement, like playing cards spread on a table. By this rhythmic arrangement, Braque attempts to compensate for the three-dimensionality of these planes, for nowhere else in the composition is there any other movement that would suggest either such distance or perspective movement.

Georges Braque, *The Table. The Museum of Modern Art, New York. Lillie P. Bliss Bequest*

Cubism was not an experiment; it was an art form of precise convention, apparently too limited to endure long as a working method in an age of endlessly changing conventions and aesthetics. Certain Cubist paintings, notably the early works of Braque and Picasso, are among the masterpieces of the world. Like all space concepts, Cubism came to fruition when interpreted by great painters.

NEO-PLASTICISM

The form construction in Mondrian's Cubist paintings is a principle whereby, from various points of projection such as

Piet Mondrian, *Composition in White, Black and Red. Collection, The Museum of Modern Art, New York. Gift of the Advisory Committee*

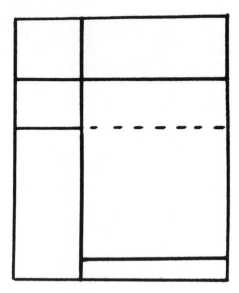

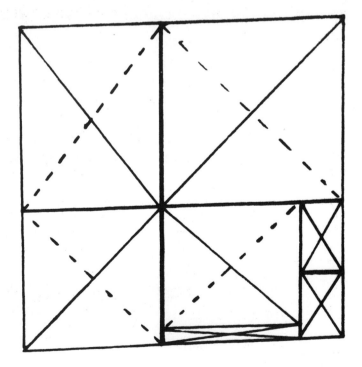

With the possible exception of a perfect sphere, all empty surfaces are imbued with implied movements. This is based on the assumption that surrounding the empty space, or void, there are lines and other directionals that can affect the void. But with the rectangle, despite the many lines that might be drawn horizontally and vertically within its surface, only two diagonal lines (forming an X) can be drawn from corner to corner. These diagonals, as far as the artist is concerned, must not be considered as a movement and a countermovement because they are equal and are not at right angles to each other. Nevertheless, in a painting that incorporates a number of rectangles of varying proportions together with their diagonal implications, it is possible for some of the diagonals to exist at right angles to each other. In fact, Mondrian's use of the implied movements through shapes is a salient factor in his compositional method, and helps bind together the horizontal and vertical movements of his rectangles. One must remember that the activity in a painting by Mondrian, culturally rooted in seventeenth-century Dutch painting, moves only in a horizontal and vertical direction—not with the varying directions of overlapping planes as in Cubism.

With Mondrian, the vertical and horizontal movements terminate in the revolving movement of a kinetic space. If the various planes in his painting cannot be seen as moving horizontally or vertically, such planes would produce a dead spot—a clogging of the movement. In Diagram 1, a tracing from a painting by Mondrian (the dotted line *is not* part of the painting) was drawn to explain the continuing direction of a line that actually ends at the first vertical bar on the left of the painting. In Diagram 2, the diagonals (which were also drawn in each rectangle) show an implied large, asymmetrical, diamond-shaped movement; apparently tilted to the right, this imparts kinetic movement to the whole picture.

In earlier works, a whole network of diagonals, probably laid out on graph paper, no doubt inspired Mondrian's placement of rectangles. In the later years of his life, Mondrian found stimulation for his compositions by pinning to the wall, in a random way, small rectangles of colored construction paper. These papers gave an impression of perspective, as might be observed in an open field upon which sign boards are placed. This three-dimensional inspiration, based on the eyes' vagrant journey, is also comparable to objects in a still life. Just as Chardin, Cézanne, or Matisse disciplined such objects onto the frontal plane, so too did Mondrian find positive vertical and horizontal placement—in his later works often inspired by colored sheets. The black and narrow planes in Mondrian's paintings—considered merely as lines by many persons—are conceived as part of Mondrian's theory of oppositions. They also serve to make more emphatic the horizontal and vertical structure. The only lines in Mondrian's works and those of most of the other neo-Plasticists, as these painters conceive it, occur at the juncture where one color meets another.

the trees he painted, there are movements in simple directions up and down, and across the surface. Because of his open method, Mondrian's canvases are not weakened by unresolved fragments of the kind observed in Gris. In his neo-Plastic paintings, for which he is best known, Mondrian even removed the illusory projection of overlapping planes, eschewing approximation for a more exact determination of space.

In other important technical considerations, Mondrian held that the strongest oppositions on the picture surface were the right angle, the primary colors, the black and white. He did not employ the circle since, in his opinion, a circle had too many chords and segments to be resolved in painting; he regarded curves and semicircles as segments of the circles.

In his youth, Mondrian was something of a nature worshipper but he was later horrified by the idea of its seductiveness, and came to fear its power as a detriment to man. He said, "The intuitive leads men upward; the instinctive leads them down and backward." Though he mistrusted mysticism and subjective ideology, preferring to advance his art on the basis of material experience, Mondrian's principle was similar to that of the mystic Meister Eckhart, who wrote, "Above all, let thought be free, for it alone stands above nature." Mondrian was opposed to any concept of monism, or any idea of the oneness of man with nature and his creator. He was concerned with man's freedom, but he did not wish this freedom to be on a subliminal level. Like Kandinsky, whose work did not appeal to him, Mondrian fell into the trap of attempting to destroy the memory of the world seen and sensed.

But Mondrian, despite his aversion to nature, in the belief that it was the tyrant of man, rejected the outright abandonment of nature in the process of his work. He said that abandoning nature in that sense was wrong and what the artist should do was to attempt to see *through* nature to the hidden truths. It was the subjectivity and neoreligious character of

Kandinsky's concept that Mondrian objected to; but despite their different approaches to the problem, both Mondrian and Kandinsky desired that their art be an instrument in freeing humanity from the oppression of the particular and the symbolic. Ironically, in his later work Kandinsky sought a new system of symbols.

There are several important schools of nonrepresentational painting in addition to the neo-Plasticism which Mondrian, Van Doesburg, and Vantongerloo personified. These include Purism (Le Corbusier and Ozenfant) and Suprematism (Lissitzky and Malevich), both movements that derive from Cubism. Both rest on a shallow space characterized by geometric subdivisions of that space.

The Purists accepted the Cubists' organization, best exemplified by Juan Gris, in their relentless search for clarity and precision of design. Nevertheless, they looked for a compromise with the general public in the portrayal of greatly simplified, though recognizable, objects. The choice of objects was restricted to such utensils as jugs, pots, pans, bottles, and the like—objects known intimately to the average Western man for centuries.

Suprematism is related to Cubism in that it has the same shallow space and superimposed planes. However, this movement was revolutionary in the concept of its practitioners who regarded the abstract means as nonrepresentational in the whole, as well as in the detail—or, in other words, the supremacy of the pure, unadorned perception of form. Kasimir Malevich's painting *White on White*—a white square set into a white background—is the best-known work of this movement; it has had a distinct influence on modern schools of applied design.

Though the works of the Constructivists are much more complex than those of the Purists, their completely nonrepresentational elements are frequently derived from such phenomena

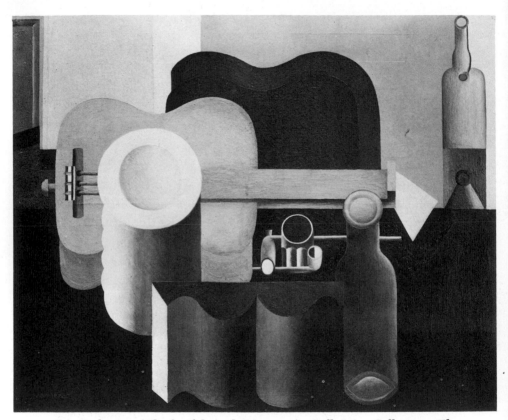

Le Corbusier (Charles-Édouard Jeanneret), *Still Life. Collection, The Museum of Modern Art, New York. Van Gogh Purchase Fund*

Juan Gris, *Guitar and Flowers. Collection, The Museum of Modern Art,* ➤ *New York. Bequest of Anna Erickson Levene*

Kasimir Malevich, *Suprematist Composition (Airplane Flying). Collection, The Museum of Modern Art, New York*

as a beam of light or the shadow of an object, as well as from images conceived in the mind. Naum Gabo and Antoine Pevsner, who were brothers, are the ablest of those artists associated with this discipline.

Artists who were in Paris during the 1920's and early 1930's may remember the straitjacket Cubism had become and the attempts artists made to escape its confining grasp. It is difficult to evaluate whether it was the methodology of Cubism or the commanding figure of Picasso, who alone seemed able to explore the wide possibilities of this system, that made it so oppressive to younger artists. Or was it that the Cubist method did not yield to any aesthetic concept structured to its own formal conventions? In fact, Picasso declared that Cubism was an art form related only to itself.

The wartime and post-World War I Dadaists really had no personal credo of artistic form. They accepted whatever in the contemporary art world best suited their purposes while the Surrealists, at least in the early formulation of the movement, admitted any idiom as long as it expressed the psychological and ideological concerns of their essentially literary bent—an ideology expressed abstractly by Miró, pseudorealistically by Dali, and magically by Magritte.

Curiously, it was the decorative Cubist period of Picasso, when he produced *The Three Musicians*, that drew the sharpest criticism, and this work, which was so intensively imitated, became the unloved symbol of Cubism. The earlier Cubistic ventures of Mondrian were not widely regarded at that time. Also, Mondrian resolved certain formal and spatial problems during his Cubist period and found another direction in abstract painting, which actually was a logical sequence of his Cubistic work. The collage methods of decorative Cubism, however, continued to be an influence, and are still very much in evidence in pop art, where the photomontage and other elements, including sculpturally projected details, are held

We shall not discuss surrealism or metaphysical painting as a formal method since the practitioners of these manners had various ways of interpreting the central principles of modern painting according to their own intentions—most of which, like Giorgio de Chirico's *The Anxious Journey*, emphasize psychological suggestion. *Collection, The Museum of Modern Art, New York. Acquired through the Lillie P. Bliss Bequest*

Chaim Soutine, *The Old Mill*. The movements in Soutine's painting appear
to be the repetitious motions of the hand that held the brush. But Soutine's rather crooked and lopsided compositions are not asymmetrical because of the lack of oppositional movements. What gives the work its
great value is the deep richness of Soutine's palette and the colors conceived in such violent, genuine motion. *Collection, The Museum of
Modern Art, New York. Vladimir Horowitz and Bernard Davis Funds*

together by the large planar divisions and accents of the picture surface.

POST-CUBIST ART

It is not an easy task to deal with the spatial and structural aspects of the post-Cubist period—that is, from 1919 until the present. Painters and sculptors are superseded almost hourly by other names. Then too, the formal aspects of art works are denigrated in value and submerged beneath the philosophical and literary subject matter of recent movements. This is often accomplished by a most persuasive and emotionally charged criticism. In spite of this, there is a certain antagonism to having much of the new art subjected to a dispassionate analysis concerning space and structure, other than what the artists themselves list in their bill of particulars.

Perhaps the most important consideration in an analysis of recent directions in painting is the way painters of different schools regard the surface of the picture. In this, there are several major groups: painters who consider the surface to be activated by the projection of planes, which is what it was to the Cubists; painters who consider the surface to be a field upon which they can create images and find an order more or less independent of their involvement with the picture surface—as did Kandinsky and Pollock; painters who see the surface as a field of operation on which they can act out their creative impulses, as with the Tachists and action painters; and finally those painters, such as Barnett Newman and Mark Rothko, who consider the surface to be a field divided into color areas, often of such magnitude that the material itself speaks directly to the observer.

There is little doubt that Kandinsky, in his mature work, saw the surface as a field; but his statement that color could not exist by itself—and that only a discernible form could do

George Byron Browne, *Azoic Fugue*. Byron Browne was one of the most prolific and searching artists of the 1930's and 1940's. Even though he is relegated to the past by contemporary critics, he is one of the proto-moderns of the later decades. Browne worked with such ease that he was never obliged to take refuge in the "cuisine" of painting, and he never attempted to impose a false stylistic unity onto his canvases, as many of the artists who followed him did, in the name of "taste." *Collection, Mrs. Oliver Baker*

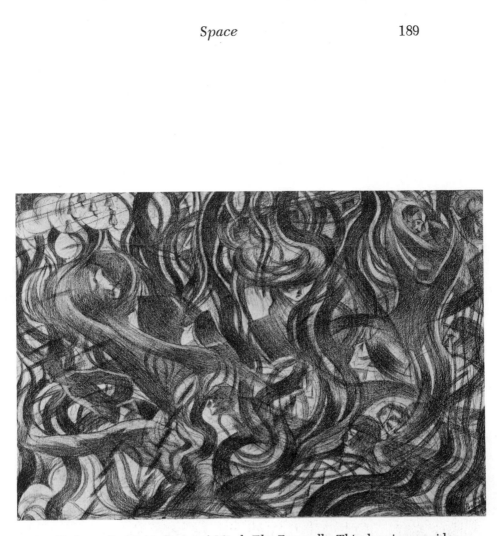

Umberto Boccioni, *States of Mind: The Farewells.* This drawing provides an evident contradiction between the serpentine design and the literal faces hidden like Easter eggs in the swirling reeds of the design. The faces of the persons, especially those in the upper right-hand section, kissing good-bye, are literally, even academically, conceived. This dichotomy between spatial and structural ideals is frequently seen in Futurist painting and is an embarrassment suffered by artists who seek both a political and artistic revolution, as the Futurists certainly did—at all costs. Only Carlo Garra seems to have solved the problem of unifying his silhouettes with the perpetual motion of Futurist space. *Collection, The Museum of Modern Art, New York. Gift of Vico Baer*

Jack Sonenberg, *Wing*. Acrylic on canvas. The philosophy of minimal art is expressed in the name. By the simplest of devices, the artists seek to bring to life the surfaces they employ. This is usually done without recourse to sentiment or memory on the part of the artist—or the observer. With Sonenberg, a simple diagonal division of black and white suffices to articulate a very large canvas. The minimal artists frequently use graph paper to find the exact proportion for the division of their surfaces. If the canvas was a melody, this operation would be comparable to a suspension in music. *Byron Gallery, New York*

Adolph Gottlieb, *Aureole. Courtesy Marlborough-Gerson Gallery, Inc., New York*

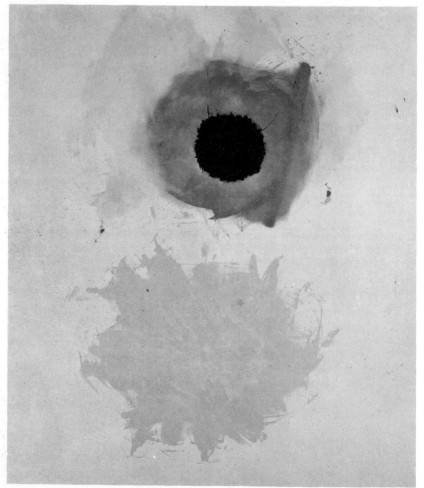

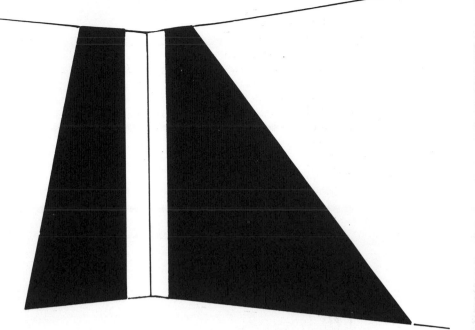

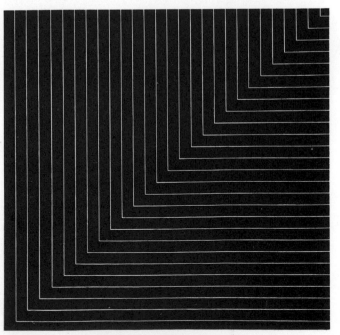

Frank Stella, *Hampton Roads*. This canvas is also minimal in character and serial in its repetition, though Stella's shaped canvases, made recently, seem to be a development of color rhythms and form extensions through the shaping of his large surfaces. *Collection, Larry Rubin, New York*

There is a phenomenal resemblance in the works of Antoni Tàpies and Alberto Burri to aerial photography—the stains and patterns of broken walls. In many ways this vision resembles art at its very origins: the respect for the mysteries of surfaces often seen in primitive art and maintained to a degree in archaic art is the basis of the Tachist vision. The most successful Tachist artists oppose the empty areas of their canvases to those areas that are richly textured, giving both areas a rather magical life and spatial quality.

Alberto Burri, *Composition Variée. Martha Jackson Gallery, New York*

Antoni Puig Tàpies, *Gray Relief on Black. Collection, Museum of Modern Art, New York. Gift of G. David Thompson*

Aerial photo

Detail of aerial photograph

Note the similarity of this detail portion of the aerial photo to the works of Burri and Tàpies.

so—focuses the limitation Kandinsky placed on both form and color. Nevertheless, he speculated that it was possible that artists might one day manipulate color so that it could attain its own autonomy.

Paul Klee was another artist who accepted the surface as a field, although in his rather cryptic sketchbook he refers to the surface as a world in which the artist could stroll either imaginatively, or even as he would in an actual walk through a park. In this case, the technical concerns of painting are subject to Klee's poetic, though very logical, definitions. He refers to drawing and other graphic elements, as the "plastic"; therefore we must assume that the image is synonymous with plasticity to Klee, who regarded the plastic as that which is graspable.

Miró is a great admirer of Klee, and Klee's imagery is in some ways comparable to his; in addition, Miró conceives the surface as a field. However, the ordering of Miró's surface elements is subject to some of the formal disciplines of Cubism. Actually, the shapes in Miró's paintings are juxtaposed, or appear to be, while the movements that unite these shapes are organized in what might casually be referred to as "peekaboo planes," because the planes, while indicated, are never drawn out or explained away.

Paul Klee, *Girl with Doll Carriage*. This is Klee at his best. ➤ An extraordinarily competent draftsman, he came to an elegance of space and design through his playful and witty caricatures. Klee imposed his drawing upon the space of the paper and actually referred to drawing as the plastic part of painting—which leads us to believe that he meant by "plastic" something to be grasped intellectually. His unerring taste made it possible for him to use the methods of caricature without making his work commonplace. And, importantly, he shared with Joan Miró the gift of knowing exactly when to stop. *Collection, The Museum of Modern Art, New York*

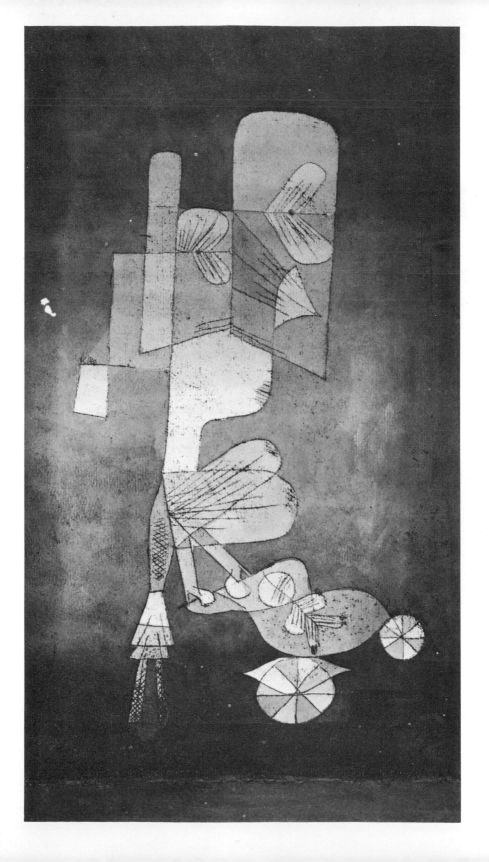

The paintings of Jackson Pollock and Mark Tobey seem filled with overlays of lines, spots, and spatters that appear as if inspired by energies comparable to those seen in the tracings of highly charged atomic particles. The methods of both painters result in such a density of surface, and such a thickening accumulation of minute elements that the surface of their paintings actually appears to be undulating: the original field ceases to exist and is reduced to an assemblage of minute particles and assumes the same character as the marks placed upon it.

If the brushstrokes of the Abstract Expressionist painters transform the surface into fields of energy, the accumulated splatter of the Tachist blots make for a similar result. On the other hand, the practice of the Tachists in ever enlarging the scale and dimension of these blots almost warrants the conclusion that they achieved a space through the unforeseen accidents that occurred in their use of various materials. With this another phenomenon took place: a dream of many modern artists was realized with the substitution of the mind-directed hand as the prime agent in painting with another order existing within man himself, and which artists, working in this method, consider comparable in quality and exactitude to one cerebrally conceived.

A shortcoming of this method is that so many of the automatically controlled paintings lack sequence, cadence, and contrast, and that the natural rhythms of the painters, born of gesture and calisthenics, cancel each other out. In the best examples of this manner, the painters must have done a certain amount of postexcitement rearranging. It is claimed that the process described resembles the procedures of Zen Buddhist artists. Actually, it resembles more the great adjustment doctrine of Sigmund Freud. There is no denying that a growth of the spirit is involved in all creativity, but thought is at least an equal partner in this activity, if not the governor.

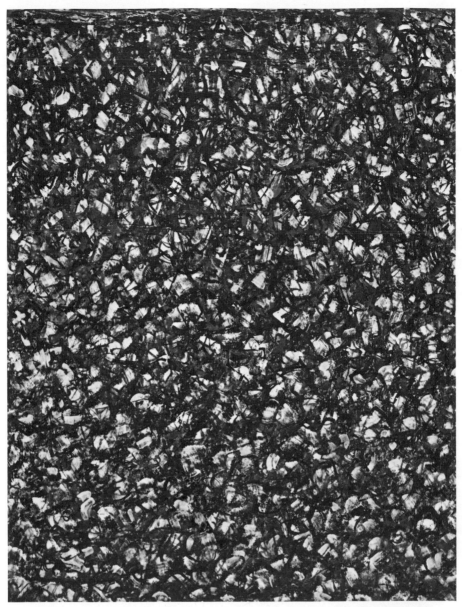

Mark Tobey, *Multiple Windows*. Tobey, like Pollock, can best be under-stood as one of the artists working with physical energies who achieves a unification of the surface with the mark drawn or painted upon it. But Tobey differs from others in this category because of his contemplative nature and the sheer poetry of his artistry. *Willard Gallery, New York. Photo, Geoffrey Clements*

Robert Motherwell, *Automatic Image #6. Courtesy Marlborough-Gerson
Gallery, Inc., New York*

Certainly the perceptive faculties of the modern artist have been enlarged and sharpened in a degree comparable to those of the artist of prehistoric times; but now this perception has emerged almost directly from the adventure of painting. The collage and blot have opened new vistas; artists have discovered in these methods things they could never otherwise have plotted or designed.

Perhaps it is because of this current imbalance between the faculty of perception and the ability to create through cerebration that the later painters of hard-edge painting and color imagery confine themselves to designs of such simplicity, for which they are sometimes accused of depletion. In spite of extravagant claims made for them of constant innovation and heroic progress, some of these artists might achieve more real esteem by simply acknowledging that they are refining and exploiting the momentous discoveries of Burgoyne Diller, Theo van Doesburg, El Lissitzky, Kasimir Malevich, and Piet Mondrian. After all, an individual artist learns only so much during his lifetime; after that his importance is established by what he accomplishes with what he learned earlier. Why shouldn't the artists who are working in a collective sense build on the findings of those who have worked, or are working, in the same idiom, without always attempting to fulfill the constant cry for further innovation?

It is not true that the art of our present decade is completely one of reduction and ultimate emptiness because some manifestations—such as hard-edge painting and optical art—appear so final in the way the works of these styles are designed. There are more lyrical and freer artists, and those, like the neo-Dadaists, who, by insisting on the purely visual, continue to broaden the visual imagination. Also, the fact that collage, montage, and Tachism can be used for purposes entirely different from those in which they were originally intended proves the depth of their possibilities.

Charles G. Shaw, *Polygon-44*. One of the pioneers of abstract art in the 1930's and still painting, Shaw can easily be seen as one of the contemporary practitioners of the simplified styles—except for the fact that he has worked, more or less, in this *avant-garde* manner for the past forty years. *Courtesy Bertha Schaefer, New York*

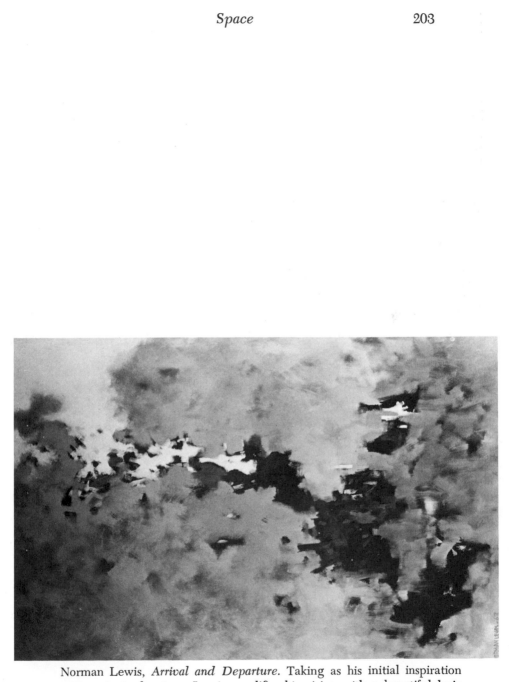

Norman Lewis, *Arrival and Departure*. Taking as his initial inspiration some aspect of nature, Lewis amplifies his vision with a beautiful lyric and abstract interpretation of his subject matter. *Willard Gallery, New York*

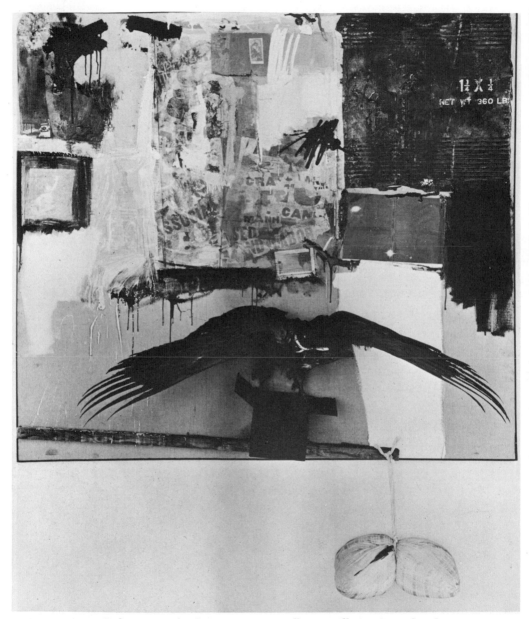

Robert Rauschenberg, *Canyon. Collection Illeana Sonnabend*

Raymond Saunders, in paintings like *Soda,* has successfully combined ➤ the techniques of pop with those of collage and painting. *Courtesy Terry Dintenfass, Inc., New York*

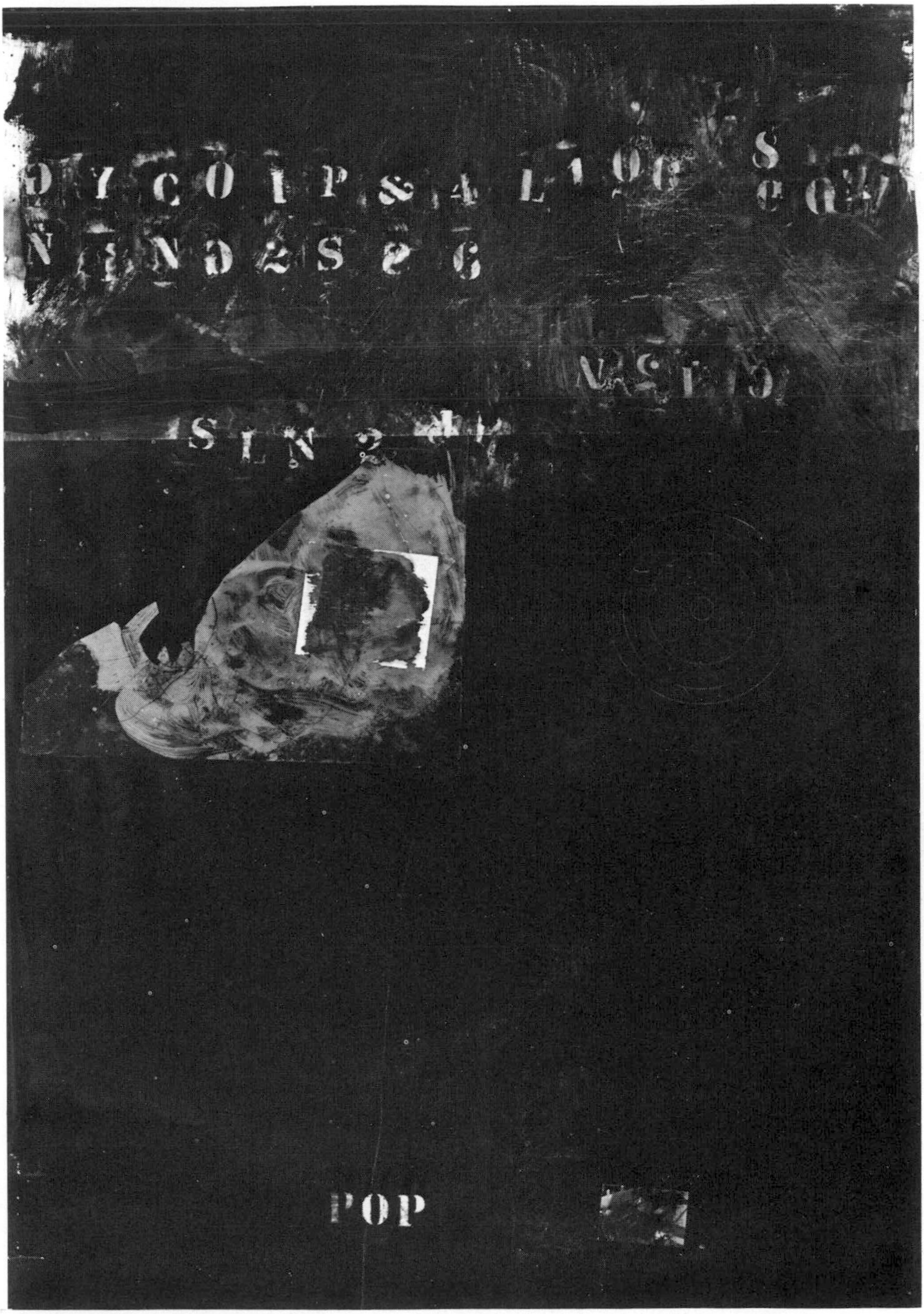
POP

Optical art, like any other art, is dependent on the limitations of human perception, and most of the examples of this genre bedazzle the eye and leave it with numerous afterimages and a feeling of visual strain. Although it is not true for the entire school, the more flamboyant examples display strong colors of almost equal chromatic strength, in which case the eye can see composedly for only a few seconds; after this, the eye is confused by the spectacle. The less aggressive paintings are arranged in bright colors and all tonal relationships are avoided. The structure of the works is generally conventional in design, often symmetrical in plan, in order that there will be no interference with the sensations provided by the colors. As one would expect, this movement has affinities with the science of optics and is sympathetic to those who are romantic about science, and who seek a direct relationship between painting and the scientific atmosphere of our life and times.

If the Tachists and devotees of concrete art invite the observer to invest the canvas with their own imagination, they do avoid the use of symbols. In other words, there are no signposts given—as with the Dadaists. Those artists who provide a symbol, whatever it may be, give a key to their works' literary meaning and content.

In his painting of recent years, Richard Lindner is one of the best exponents of this trend through the directness and clarity of his exposition. The contrasts and textural oppositions, such as the round softness of the figures, which are opposed to objects of a mechanical shape and character, augment his symbolic drama. Such mechanics are often employed by the Surrealists, who, however, used more disparate combinations of objects and symbols. A newer school, with which Lindner has affinities, combines the exactness of the "new objectivity" (*Neue Sachlichkeit*) with the machinery extracted from Léger's period of mechanical art. But Lindner very often uses symbols of the motion picture and of our motorcycle society, and he

Roy Lichtenstein, *Night Seascape. Courtesy Leo Castelli, New York*

Jacob Lawrence, *Flower Woman*. For years Lawrence has been one of the important modern "social" painters, along with Jack Levine, William Gropper, and others. *Courtesy Terry Dintenfass, Inc., New York*

◄ Richard Lindner, *Coney Island #2. Photo, Geoffrey Clements. Courtesy, Cordier and Ekstrom, Inc., New York*

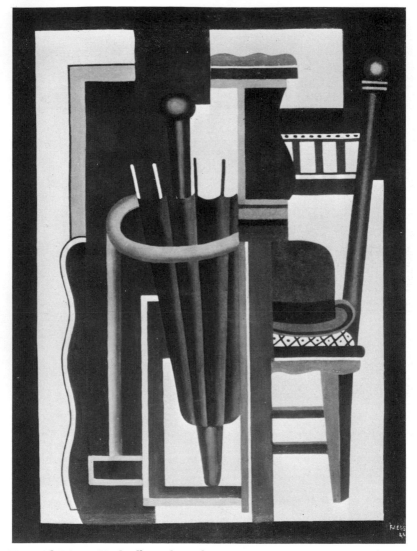

Fernand Léger, *Umbrella and Bowler.* Here Léger attempts to synthesize more firmly the design of the fractured paintings of perhaps his greatest period—that known as "paysage animée," which terminated in his great painting *The City.* The objects remain, but they are pressed into a flatter and more ornamental space. There are deliberate contrasts of rounded and flat contours, curved and straight lines, modeled and flat surfaces— all of which are related in three-dimensional rhythms sufficiently scattered to be lost in the two-dimensionality of a monumental plan. Note how the objects depicted, like those of the Purists, are simple and commonly known—to provide a link between what the viewer easily understands and the "new space." *The Museum of Modern Art, New York. A. Conger Goodyear Fund*

Standard Brand #2 emphasizes a vital facet of Stuart Davis's work—the use of lettered and written words as part of his compositional structure. Because of this technique, Davis is seen by some persons as a progenitor of many of today's Pop artists. The words in Davis's paintings, though, are much easier to comprehend than the sophisticated plastic language of his pictorial conceptions. He felt the need to relate his works to the popular jazz idiom and current myths of his time, much like Léger related his work to the city and to the machine. Here Davis uses words in two languages to add yet another element to the poetry of his word-and-form structure. *Collection of Mrs. Stuart Davis*

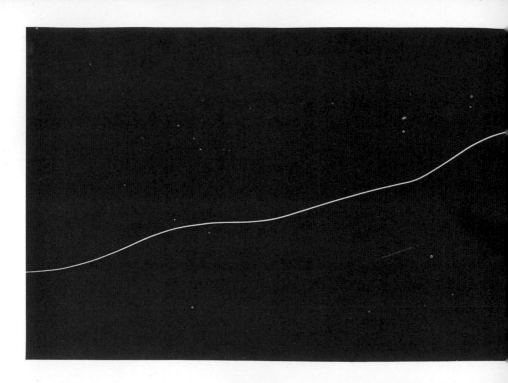

David Budd, *Typhoon.* While using methods employed by the minimal artists, Budd's work, however, has a "transactional" intention. It is the carrier of an idea—in this painting an idea inspired by Conrad's novel *Typhoon. Photo by Rudolph Burckhardt*

Andy Warhol, *Flowers. Courtesy Leo Castelli, New York*

has created, in his exotic female figures, almost a prototype of the modern goddess.

There are so many borderline cases, and artists who combine features of several styles, that it is almost impossible to identify the practitioners of all the various contemporary mannerisms. However, no matter what its particular characteristics, no contemporary painting can have failed to be influenced by some of the spatial concepts we have outlined.

Wyndham Lewis claims that the action philosophy of Henri Bergson has so permeated our thought that we see all things as relative and easy to manipulate. The hardware, the comic strips, and the labels of old soup cans used by the pop artist are poor symbols for what is the real "junk" of today. Yet in another sense, today's Philistine sees in these mannerisms of romantic decay an excuse for his own desires to live on a luxurious level, and dream at the same time of the jukebox and the honky-tonks. There is a great difference between the pop art of today and what some people have incorrectly considered its equivalent in the nineteenth century—the cult of the "beautiful ugly," as espoused by Courbet. In the last century this cult was a revolt against the sweetness of the academy, while today it *is* the academy itself.

If it seems that there are more startling than definitive developments in the spatial adventure of contemporary painting, this is because a new style is possible only through the combined vision of the painter and that of society at a given moment in history. Even if the painter is a precursor (as were Cézanne, Michelangelo, and Giotto), he does not come to his statement through any power of divination.

If traditional methods and objectives have lost their meaning, where can the painter turn? We know that he must base his art on discovery and on protracted study; he cannot, as he was often able to in the past, come into a ready-made style. Yet there are those who admonish the painter to represent the world as it is. The people who ask for this reality give the painter, or the sculptor, little spiritual certitude of the reality they claim to have in mind.

There are, however, positive factors. At no time in history has the art of all the world been so available to artists—at least through such information as reproductions can furnish, in what. Malraux refers to as "the museum without walls." The possibilities for the artist seem endless, his choices and points of departure infinite. The painter stands in a paradoxical relation to life and to the space in which life is lived. The painted image as transposed by the painter may have only a passing resemblance to what in life inspired the image, but then may have a meaning far beyond what was intended. Ultimately, of course, those images of lasting value will incorporate, within the personal response to order, a lucidity of intention, structure, and spatial arrangement.

IV

The
Artist's
Maturation

Although we have related our study of space and structure to the painter's deep reflection, some of his working methods may not have originated solely in his conscious thought. These procedures were perfected and applied over the years and were the result of intensive trial and error and of percipient deliberation. Nevertheless, we are aware of the limitation of any method; we realize there are greater truths toward which any methodology is only a stepping-stone.

We could have chosen other elements of art for extended analysis—design, pattern, or chiaroscuro, for instance—rather than space or structure. But space is not such an element: it is the environment of a work of art, and as such is in effect the world in which the work exists. The artist himself, we also must remember, exists in space, and he seeks to rationalize it throughout his artistic life.

Structure is the anatomy of space, but it also represents the total investment of the artist; the vehicle of his means, and the filter of his inspiration and imagination. In the end, in a completely realized work, space and structure become one.

As we have demonstrated, artists who worked within the great historical styles accepted certain formal principles that ordered every aspect of their art. And we can observe in the works of these artists certain construction devices and methods of operation that are still useful. Yet despite the overwhelming collective power of the great styles, the masters who worked within the formal content of these styles had spatial identities peculiar to themselves. What distinguishes every great artist, in fact, is the spatial world in which he and his art exist. This spatial identity is a culmination of all the influences of his time, his life, and his way of seeing the world.

In attempting to trace an artist's development through maturity, we might compare his progress to the four ages of man: childhood, youth, manhood, and finally old age. The four stages of an artist's life are not dissimilar, though they are grouped rather differently. Childhood and youth are seen as one—that is, a period of learning. Manhood can be classified in two stages: at first when the artist works free from the formal instruction of his teachers, until that time when he breaks through to a mastery of his craft. In the last stage, by means of great perseverance, wisdom, and drive, the artist learns to accept the limitations of both his medium and himself, and finds a true relation with his art. He is then able to see both the inner and outer world of his creation with the same intensity, so that the total structure of his work is an outcome of his own effort and vision.

This view of the artist's royal road to maturity and triumph is, of course, the ideal, and it is in no way related to physical chronology. A period of great attainment, as with Castagno, Raphael, and Seurat, is frequently arrived at early in life—especially, it appears, with those geniuses fated to die young.

Of these three great painters, Raphael, who died in his thirty-seventh year had the longest life-span.

Nor do only the most mature artists create works of artistic merit. Young artists, carried on the wings of spontaneity and enthusiasm, are often the innovators and heralds of new styles. We think immediately of Impressionists like Bazille, Monet, and Renoir, who in their youth explored new insights into form and color, and, in recent years, of Braque and Picasso, whose early Cubist paintings a number of persons consider their best work.

But in the old age of the truly gifted artist, unique and wonderful things often occur. This is especially true of the drawings of such artists, when in this medium a universality of perception unifies and brings into rapport artists of the most diverse cultures. For example, we see in the late watercolors of Cézanne affinities with Sung painters; in Ingres' pencil drawings a veneration of the classic line of Raphael; and in Klee, a graphic relationship with ancient calligraphers. Together with the drawings, the other late works of the great masters have a simplicity that often makes us wonder at the very majesty of something that should appear commonplace. The striving for originality, the pursuit of skills for their own sake, and all other irrelevancies disappear. The master artist tends to forego surface refinements and to abjure all that is not of the deep wisdom of poetry. Secure in his space and structure, he is at one with the world he was born into and that world of difficulties he has overcome, and can now be seen for what he truly represents.

Index

(italicized page numbers indicate illustrations)

219